Creating MLA Style Research Papers

Using Microsoft Word 97

Steven Forsythe

Author

Brea, California

StevensPress

P. O. Box 1795, Brea, CA 92822-1795

http://www.stevenspress.com

StevensPress

Credits

Cover Artist: Bernice Howard
Editors: Marilyn Martin and Nancy Forsythe
Book Design and Layout: David Bonnewitz
Cover Design: David Bonnewitz
Production Manager: Stephen Howard
Author: Steven Forsythe

StevensPress

Registered Trademarks

Microsoft® Word is a registered trademark of Microsoft Corporation
MLA® is a registered trademark of the Modern Language Association

ISBN 0-9670741-0-X
© Copyright 1999 **Stevens**Press

Printed in the United States

0 9 8 7 6 5 4 3 2 1

TABLE OF CONTENTS

To the Instructor

At some point, every college student will be required to write a research paper using the Modern Language Association (MLA) style. As a teacher, you may explain these guidelines in your classroom or refer your students to a book in the library or to a bookstore where you may purchase a book that contains the complete MLA style guidelines. In the process of writing a research paper, the student will have to word process the paper using a word processing program and a personal computer. Depending upon the computer skill level of your students, the task of word processing a research paper may be a time-consuming and frustrating experience.

This book contains a sample research paper and the steps to follow to create the paper. Students can create the sample research paper or use the steps as a guideline to create their own research paper. The book contains over ninety screen captures, allowing students to perform a step and then compare the results on their computer to the screen capture in the book.

This book consists of three sections: 1) Creating a Research Paper; 2) Editing a Research Paper; and 3) Appendixes. In the first section, students create a sample research paper using Microsoft Word 97. In the process, students learn to change page margins and line spacing, create a running head to number the pages, type parenthetical citations, insert a table, create references on the Works Cited page, determine the word count, use the tools to spell check and grammar check the paper, and save and print the paper.

Although the MLA style suggests the use of parenthetical citations instead of footnotes, some disciplines (art, history, music, religion, theology, and history) continue to use footnotes to document their sources. To accommodate these disciplines, the research paper contains a footnote and the steps to create a footnote. After reading this book, students will understand how to use parenthetical citations and footnotes. The entire sample research paper is shown in Figure 1 on pages 2 and 3.

The second section, Editing a Research Paper, illustrates how to make changes to the research paper. In the process, the student will learn to navigate within the multiple page research paper, find and replace text, insert and delete text, undo a previously performed operation, use the Word Thesaurus, and obtain help.

The third section contains two appendixes. Appendix A contains the MLA style guidelines and Microsoft Word default settings. Appendix B contains the general steps to create a research paper.

This book was written so that a student with limited computer skills can follow the steps on a computer in the computer lab or on their personal computer. However, you may want to demonstrate how to word process the sample research paper in this book in a classroom demonstration. With practice and a minimal amount of equipment, you can easily demonstrate how to create the research paper in a 50-minute class period.

For additional information, follow the steps below to connect to our Web site.

StevensPress Web Site

For additional information, teaching tips and techniques, links to other Web sites, or to communicate with the publishing company or author, visit our Web site. The Web site contains additional information for the students that is not available in the book. To view the Web site, follow the steps below:

1. Turn on your computer.
2. Start your Web browser software (Internet Explorer or Netscape).
3. Type in the Web site address (http://www.stevenspress.com) in the Location box (Netscape) or Address box (Internet Explorer) and press the ENTER key.
4. Click the Instructor button or Student button to view additional pages in the Web site.

To the Student

Most students entering college today have previously taken a word processing class and are required to take a college-level English composition course. Typically, this course teaches the basics of English usage and grammar, explains the methodology for writing research papers and contains an exposure to the Modern Language Association (MLA) guidelines for creating research papers. However, many courses do not show how to word process a research paper.

This book contains the steps to create and edit a sample research paper using the MLA guidelines and Microsoft® Word, a popular word processing program. The sample research paper is shown in Figure 1 on pages 2 and 3. Ninety screen captures throughout the book allow you to perform a step and then compare the results on your computer to the screen capture in the book.

The first section of this book contains the steps to create the sample research paper. In the process, you change page margins, change line spacing, create a running head to number the pages, type parenthetical citations, insert a footnote, insert a table, create references on the Works Cited page, determine the word count, spell check and grammar check the paper, and then save and print the paper.

The second section of the book contains the steps to edit the research paper. You learn to scroll a document, find and replace text, insert and delete text, undo a previously performed operation, use the Word Thesaurus, and obtain help.

The third section contains two appendixes. Appendix A contains the MLA style guidelines and Microsoft Word default settings. Appendix B contains the general steps to create a research paper.

For additional information, follow the steps below to connect to our Web site.

StevensPress Web Site

Information about MLA guidelines, links to other Web pages, and information not covered in this book are available on our Web site. To view our Web site, follow the steps below:

1. Turn on your computer.
2. Start your Web browser software (Internet Explorer or Netscape).
3. Type in the Web site address (http://www.stevenspress.com) in the Location box (Netscape) or Address box (Internet Explorer) and press the ENTER key.
4. Click the Student button to view additional pages in the Web site.

Creating a Research Paper

Chances are good that in your first year of college a teacher will ask you to write a research paper using the guidelines recommended by the Modern Language Association (MLA). The professor may explain these guidelines in a classroom lecture or simply refer you to a book in the library or to the bookstore where you can purchase a book that contains the guidelines. MLA publications may also be ordered from the organization's Web site.

The teacher will then expect you to use a computer in the school's computer lab or your own personal computer to create the research paper. This book contains the steps to create a research paper using the MLA guidelines and Microsoft® Word 97, a popular word processing program. Follow these steps to create the sample research paper illustrated in this book or to create a research paper of your choosing.

The Modern Language Association (MLA)

The **Modern Language Association (MLA)**® is a non-profit organization whose members have promoted teaching and scholarship in modern languages and literature for over a century. Through its members, the Modern Language Association encourages high standards for teaching and research, publishes various books and journals for teachers and students, and maintains a set of recommendations for preparing student research papers.

These recommendations, collectively called the **MLA documentation style**, or **MLA style**, establish guidelines for the mechanics of writing (spelling, punctuation, quotations, and form) and the documentation of **sources** (magazines, books, articles, and the like). The MLA style is widely used by teachers, schools, scholarly and literary journals, newsletters, and magazines throughout the United States. This book explains these guidelines as required to create a research paper.

Microsoft Word 97

A word processing program allows you to compose and permanently store a document on a disk, easily make changes to the document, and produce a professional looking final product. Today, more people use Microsoft Word to produce personal and business documents than any other word processor. This book illustrates how to use the most recent version of Microsoft Word, Microsoft Word 97, to create a research paper. You can purchase Microsoft Word 97 separately or as part of the Microsoft® Office 97 suite of programs. Before starting Microsoft Word 97, you must start the computer's operating system by turning on your computer.

The Sample Research Paper

Figure 1 on pages 2 and 3 illustrates the sample research paper that was prepared using the MLA style and Microsoft Word 97. The research paper, titled "Locating Sources for a Research Paper," provides information about locating sources you can use when creating a research paper. The research paper is three pages in length, containing approximately 500 words of text and a Works Cited page.

An explanatory note, or **footnote**, displays at the bottom of page one to further explain a portion of the text. A **table** containing a list of Internet resources and their descriptions displays on page 2 of the research paper.

Parenthetical citations display throughout the research paper to identify the ideas, words, or facts of another individual as they appear in the composition. A corresponding reference occurs on the Works Cited page. The **Works Cited list** on page 3 is an alphabetized list of the magazine articles, books, newspaper articles, the Internet, and other sources used in the preparation of the research paper. These works are called **references**. The Works Cited list appears on a separate page from the text of the research paper.

Although the MLA style suggests the use of parenthetical citations instead of footnotes, both footnotes and parenthetical citations are shown in the research paper. Check with your teacher to determine whether you should use parenthetical citations, footnotes, or a combination of both in your research paper.

Forsythe 1

Steven Forsythe

Professor Susan Kirkwood

English Composition 101

August 17, 2000

Locating Sources for a Research Paper ◄— research paper title

Numerous sources are available for obtaining information when writing a research paper. Among the sources, which are categorized as primary sources and secondary sources, are novels, biographies, autobiographies, documentaries, interviews, and articles from an encyclopedia.

A primary source is an original work created by an author. As such, it is more accurate than a secondary source. An autobiography, an interview you conduct, a novel, a play, or a speech is a primary source. A secondary source is an interpretation of a primary source. As such, it can be biased and inaccurate. A review, a biography, a documentary, or an article from an encyclopedia is a secondary source (Williams 57). ◄— parenthetical citation

Finding useful information for a research paper is a learned skill. Over time, a good researcher learns where to find the best sources based upon the kind of information he or she needs. For example, a good place to look for books, newspapers and journal articles, and novels may be your library. However, a library may not be the best place to find government documents and databases. The best source for this information is the Internet.[1] ◄— footnote number

The first step in locating information for your research paper is to determine the sources available, where they are located, and how to use them. Visit the library. Investigate local community services including the Chamber of Commerce, nonprofit organizations, and social service agencies. Conduct interviews and surveys to obtain firsthand information. Familiarize

_____

[1] Although the Internet is a convenient and highly accessible source of information, you should evaluate each Internet source carefully for accuracy and reliability.

footnote

Figure 1

Forsythe 2

yourself with the Internet and its resources. Table 1 contains a list of popular Internet resources, their Internet addresses, and descriptions of the resources (Anderson, 12 Mar. 2000).

parenthetical citation

Table 1

Internet Resources and Their Descriptions

Internet Resources	Descriptions
Yahoo (www.yahoo.com)	A Directory of Web Sites Organized by Topic
AltaVista (www.altavista.digital.com)	Uses Keywords to Search for Web Pages
Gopher (gopher://gopher.nara.gov)	A Menu-Driven File Retrieval System

table

As you locate sources, compile a working bibliography. Each time you locate a source you want to read, make an entry for the source on a 3" x 5" card (Howard 194-196). Even though you may not include each entry from the working bibliography in the finished research paper, each entry should contain all the information you will need to create a bibliography entry.

parenthetical citation

Finally, read each source and decide which sources to include in your research paper. The time you spend investigating, locating, and reading the sources will organize your thoughts and make the next phase, preparing the first draft of your research paper, easier.

Forsythe 3

Works Cited

Anderson, Peter. "Popular Internet Resources." Internet Research Journal 4 (1999). 12 Mar. 2000
    <http://www.irj.com>.

references in Works Cited list

Howard, Stanley. Creating a Working Bibliography. Fort Lauderdale: Literary Press, 1999.

Williams, Susan. "Locating and Evaluating Primary and Secondary Sources." Writer's Monthly
    17 Oct. 1998: 57.

Figure 1 (Continued)

The Microsoft Windows 98 Operating System

Most computers sold today include some version of the Microsoft Windows operating system. **Microsoft® Windows** controls the operation of your computer, allowing you to communicate with the computer and start application programs, such as Microsoft Word. Although different computers may use different versions of Microsoft Windows, this book illustrates Microsoft Windows 98. The following section explains how to start the Microsoft Windows 98 operating system.

Starting Microsoft Windows

Before you can use your computer to perform such tasks as creating a research paper, you must start Microsoft Windows. The following step starts Microsoft Windows and displays the Windows desktop.

Step 1 Turn on the computer.

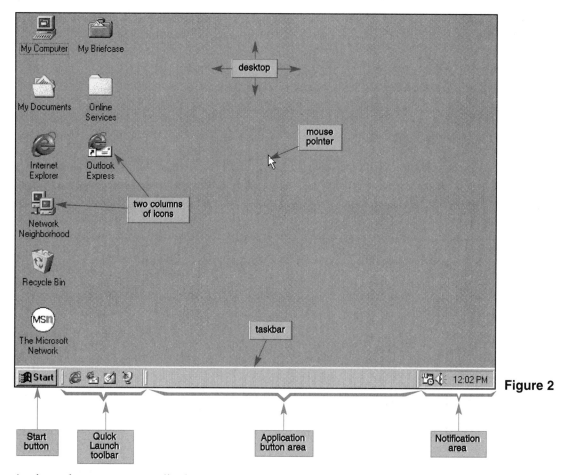

Figure 2

An introductory screen displays momentarily, and then the desktop shown in Figure 2 displays.

The **desktop** in Figure 2 contains two columns of **icons** along the left side of the desktop and a **taskbar** at the bottom. A picture and title identify each icon on the desktop. Because users often customize the desktop, the icons on the desktop and the desktop color may be different on your computer.

The taskbar at the bottom of the desktop contains the Start button, Quick Launch toolbar, Application button area, and Notification area. The **Start button** allows you to start a software program, open a new or existing document, obtain help, and shut down the computer.

The **Quick Launch toolbar** contains four icons that allow you to browse the Internet, receive and send e-mail messages, remove unwanted objects from the desktop, and view channels on the Internet. The Quick Launch toolbar on your desktop may contain a different collection of icons.

The **Application button area** contains **taskbar buttons** that correspond to open windows on the desktop. The taskbar buttons allow you to switch easily between open windows on the desktop. In Figure 2, no open windows display on the desktop, and no buttons display in the Application button area.

The **Notification area** shown in Figure 2 contains two icons and the current time. These icons allow you to schedule daily tasks and control the volume level. The icons on your computer may be different. The **taskbar clock** containing the current time (12:02 PM) displays to the right of the icons.

The **mouse pointer**, located in the center of the desktop, moves across the desktop when you move the mouse and changes shape when you point to different areas on the desktop.

The instructions to create the research paper described in this book assume you can perform the following six mouse operations: point, click, right-click, double-click, drag, and right-drag. If you have never used a mouse, ask your teacher to suggest methods to practice these mouse operations.

Starting Microsoft Word 97

The first step in preparing a research paper is to start Microsoft Word 97. To do this, you use the mouse to point, click, and double-click. **Point** means move the mouse across a surface, such as a desk, to position the mouse pointer on the desired object on the desktop. To **click**, you press and release the left mouse button. Quickly press and release the left mouse button twice to **double-click**.

Ask your teacher how to start Word on your computer, or use the following steps to start Microsoft Word 97.

Step 1 **Point to the Start button on the taskbar.**

Figure 3

The mouse pointer points to the Start button and a ScreenTip containing the text, Click here to begin, displays.

Step 2 Click the Start button.
Point to the New Office Document command on the
Start menu.

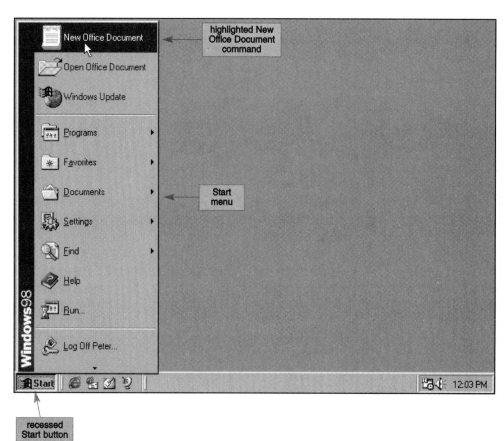

Figure 4

When you click the Start button, the Start menu displays, and the Start button recesses. A **menu** is a collection of related commands, and each **command** performs a specific task. When you point to the New Office Document command, Windows highlights the command. The commands on the Start menu may be different on your computer.

Step 3 Click the New Office Document command.
Point to the Blank Document icon in the New Office
Document dialog box.

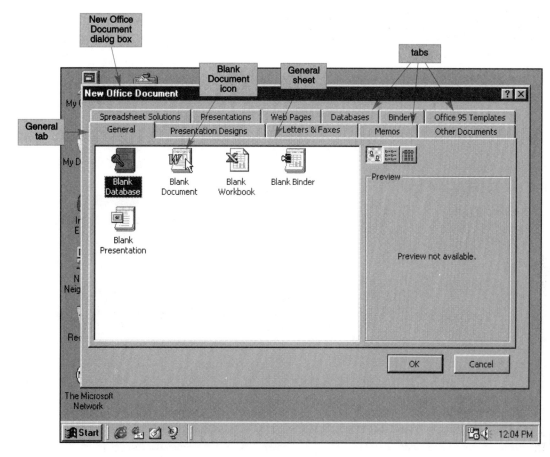

Figure 5

The Start menu disappears, and the New Office Document dialog box opens.
A **dialog box** opens to convey information or request a response. Several tabs
and the General sheet associated with the General tab display in the dialog
box. The mouse pointer points to the highlighted Blank Document icon.

Step 4 Double-click the Blank Document icon by quickly pressing and releasing the left mouse button twice.

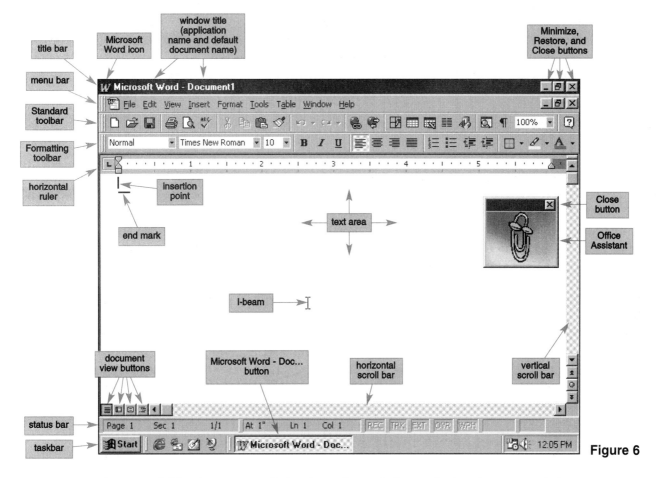

Figure 6

The New Office Document dialog box closes, Microsoft Word starts, and the maximized Microsoft Word - Document1 window opens.

The maximized Microsoft Word - Document1 window in Figure 6 fills the desktop and the Microsoft Word - Doc... button displays on the taskbar. The **title bar** contains the Microsoft Word icon and window title (Microsoft Word - Document1). The window title consists of the **application name** (Microsoft Word), a hyphen (-), and **default document name** (Document1).

The three buttons to the far right on the title bar (Minimize, Restore, and Close) allow you to manipulate the size of the window. The **Minimize button** closes the window while leaving the taskbar button on the taskbar, the **Restore button** restores the window to its smaller, original size, and the **Close button** closes the window and removes the taskbar button from the taskbar.

The **menu bar** contains nine menu names. One underlined letter appears in each menu name. You view the commands on a menu by clicking the menu name or holding down the ALT key on the keyboard and pressing the keyboard key corresponding to the underlined character in the menu name.

Below the menu bar are the Standard toolbar and Formatting toolbar. The buttons and boxes on the **Standard toolbar** allow you to perform operations such as saving and printing a document. The buttons and boxes on the **Formatting toolbar** allow you to format the text in a document and display the choices you have made.

Below the Formatting toolbar is the **horizontal ruler**, or **ruler**. The ruler allows you to set tabs, indent paragraphs, and change page margins. Below the ruler is the **text area** that displays the text you type into the document. The **insertion point** (blinking vertical line) indicates where the text you type will display in the text area. The **end mark** (horizontal line) indicates the end of the document. As you type, the end mark moves down the page.

When you point to different areas of a window or the desktop, the mouse pointer changes shape to indicate a change in function. The normal mouse pointer **(left-pointing white arrow)** indicates you can point to objects using the mouse pointer. When you point to the text area, the mouse pointer changes to an **I-beam** to indicate you can enter text.

The Office Assistant displays in the text area when you start Microsoft Word. The **Office Assistant** is one of many Help features that answer questions, offer tips, and provide Help on a variety of Word features. Click the Close button in the upper right corner of the Office Assistant window to remove the Office Assistant.

The Microsoft Word - Document1 window contains two scroll bars: a horizontal scroll bar and a vertical scroll bar. Scroll bars display when the entire document is not visible in a window. A **vertical scroll bar** contains an **up scroll arrow**, a **scroll box,** and a **down scroll arrow**. Similarly, a **horizontal scroll bar** contains a **left scroll arrow**, **scroll box**, and **right scroll arrow**. You can scroll a window in three ways: (1) click the scroll bar; (2) click the scroll arrows or hold them down for a period of time; or (3) drag the scroll box.

To the left of the horizontal scroll bar are four buttons that allow you to change the document view (Normal view, Online Layout view, Page Layout view, and Outline view). The recessed Normal view button (first button) indicates the current view is the Normal view. The **Normal view** is the preferred view when you type, edit, and format text. If another button is recessed, click the Normal view button to change to the Normal view.

The **status bar** at the bottom of the window displays various pieces of information about the document in the text area. This information as shown in Figure 6 indicates the insertion point is located on page one (Page 1), one inch from the top edge of the paper (At 1"), and one inch from the left edge of the paper (Ln 1).

Microsoft Word Default Settings

When you start Microsoft Word, the program uses pre-established settings, called **default settings**, to control the way a document looks on the screen and prints on the printer. These default settings control the page margins, text appearance and size, line spacing, and text justification. Although Word uses many default settings, you can easily change these settings to conform to the MLA guidelines. This book explains the changes required to create the research paper.

Changing the Left and Right Margins

A **page margin** is the blank space between the edge of the paper and the text in the document. Each printed page has four page margins (top, bottom, left, and right). The MLA style requires all page margins in a research paper to be one inch. The **default page margins** are a 1-inch top and bottom margin and a 1.25-inch left and right margin.

To conform to the MLA guidelines, you must change the left and right page margins from 1.25 inch to 1 inch. The following steps change the left and right margins.

Step 1   Click File on the menu bar.
Point to the Page Setup command on the File menu.

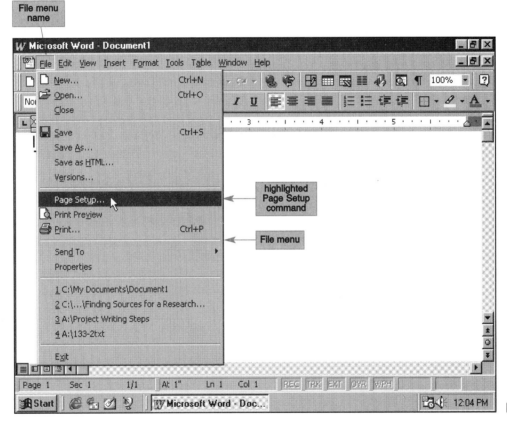

Figure 7

The File menu displays, and the mouse pointer points to the highlighted Page Setup command. An **ellipsis** (...) to the right of the Page Setup command indicates some other action can be taken when the command is clicked. In this case, a dialog box will open when you click the command.

Step 2 Click the Page Setup command.
Point to the down arrow button in the Left box.

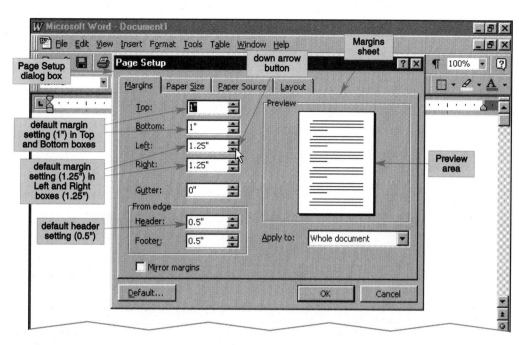

Figure 8

The Margins sheet displays in the Page Setup dialog box. The Top and Bottom boxes contain the default top and bottom margin settings (1"), the Left and Right boxes contain the default left and right margin settings (1.25"), the Preview area illustrates the default page margins, and the top margin setting is highlighted in the Top box. The mouse pointer points to the down arrow button in the Left box.

Step 3 Click the down arrow button three times to display 1" in the Left box.
Point to the down arrow button in the Right box.

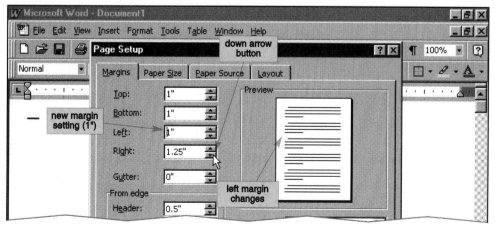

Figure 9

The Left box contains the MLA left margin guideline (1"), the left margin in the Preview area reflects the change to the left margin, and the mouse pointer points to the down arrow button in the Right box.

Step 4 Click the down arrow button three times to display 1" in the Right box.
Point to the OK button in the Page Setup dialog box.

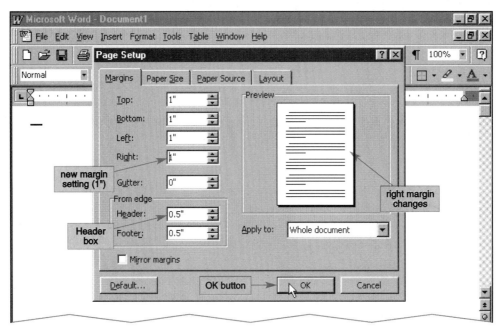

Figure 10

The Right box contains the MLA right margin guideline (1"), the right margin in the Preview area reflects the change to the right margin, and the mouse pointer points to the OK button.

Step 5 Click the OK button.

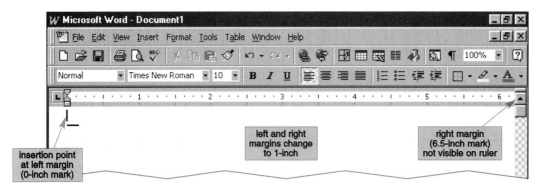

Figure 11

The left and right margins of the document change to 1 inch, the insertion point displays at the 0-inch mark (left margin), and the right margin is not visible on the ruler.

The left and right margins change from 1.25 inch to 1 inch to conform to the MLA guidelines, and the left and right margin markers on the ruler reflect the margin change. The 0-inch mark on the ruler identifies the right side of the left margin of the page. Although not visible on the horizontal ruler, the 6.5-inch mark on the ruler identifies the beginning of the right margin. These settings indicate the space between the margins is 6.5 inches. Add this amount to the one-inch margins set in the Page Setup dialog box (8.5 = 6.5 + 1 + 1), and you will see this is the correct placement on an 8.5-inch wide piece of paper.

In Figure 10 on the previous page, the default setting for the distance from the top edge of the paper to a header (0.5") displays in the Header box in the Page Setup dialog box. Later in this book, you will create a header (running head) to contain your last name and a page number. The MLA guidelines specify that the header should display one-half inch (½") from the top edge of the paper. The **default header setting** in the Header box satisfies this MLA guideline.

Changing the Zoom Setting

On some computers, changing the left and right margins causes the right margin marker and the end of each line of text entered into the document to extend beyond the visible text area. Changing the default zoom setting from 100% to Page Width causes the right margin and hidden text to display in the text area. Perform the following steps to change the zoom setting.

Step 1   Point to the down arrow button in the Zoom drop-down list box.

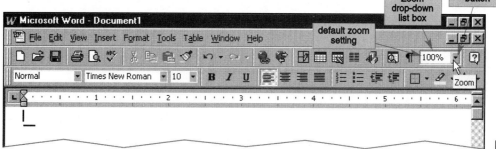

Figure 12

The mouse pointer points to the down arrow button in the Zoom drop-down list box. A **drop-down list box** consists of a box and a down arrow button. Clicking the down arrow button displays a drop-down list.

Step 2   Click the down arrow button in the Zoom drop-down list box.
Point to the Page Width setting in the Zoom drop-down list.

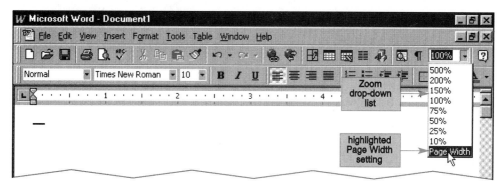

Figure 13

Word highlights the default zoom setting (100%) in the Zoom drop-down list box, displays the Zoom drop-down list, and highlights the Page Width setting in the Zoom drop-down list.

Step 3 **Click the Page Width setting.**

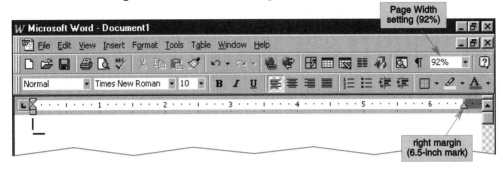

Figure 14

The right margin displays on the horizontal ruler at the 6.5-inch mark. The Page Width setting (92%) displays in the Zoom drop-down list box. The zoom setting may be different on your computer.

Changing the Font Size

Font is the term used to describe a collection of characters, numbers, and symbols with a common appearance. Another word used to describe a font is **typeface**. The **default font** is Times New Roman. **Font size** is a measure of the size of a character. The **default font size** is the 10-point font size. The default font name displays in the Font drop-down list box, and the font size displays in the Font Size drop-down list box on the Formatting toolbar (see Figure 15 below).

The MLA guidelines suggest using an easily readable font and font size. The Times New Roman font is a common choice for books and magazines in which large blocks of text are involved. As such, the Times New Roman font is an acceptable font for a research paper. An acceptable font size for preparing most business documents, including research papers, is 12 point.

To conform to the MLA guideline for font and font size, use the default Times New Roman font and change the font size from 10 point to 12 point. The following steps change the font size.

Step 1 **Point to the down arrow button in the Font Size drop-down list box on the Formatting toolbar.**

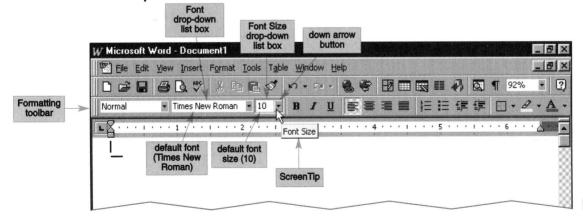

Figure 15

The Times New Roman font name displays in the Font drop-down list box, and the number 10, representing the default font size 10, displays in the Font Size drop-down list box. The mouse pointer points to the down arrow button in the Font Size drop-down list box, and a ScreenTip displays.

Step 2   Click the down arrow button to display the Font
         Size drop-down list.
         Point to 12 in the Font Size drop-down list.

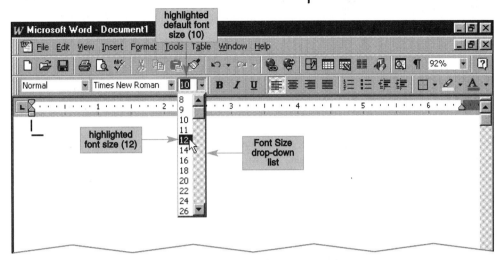

Figure 16

Word highlights the default font size (10) in the Font Size drop-down list box, displays the Font Size drop-down list, and highlights the number 12 in the Font Size drop-down list.

Step 3   Click 12 in the Font Size drop-down list.

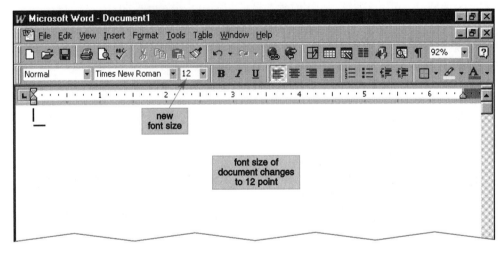

Figure 17

The number 12 displays in the Font Size drop-down list box, and the font size for the document changes to 12 point.

Changing the Line Spacing

Line spacing is the amount of vertical space between the lines of text in a document. The **default line spacing setting** is single (single spacing). Unless you change the line spacing, all lines of text in a document will be single-spaced. The MLA guidelines require the research paper to be double-spaced. The steps on the next three pages change the line spacing from single to double.

Step 1 Click Format on the menu bar.
Point to the Paragraph command on the Format menu.

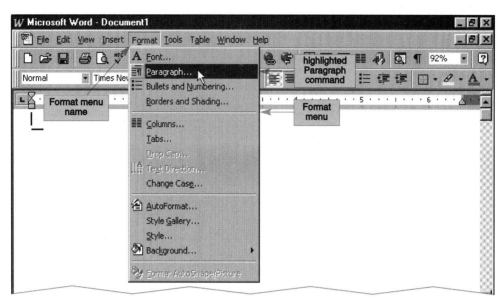

Figure 18

The Format menu displays, and the mouse pointer points to the highlighted Paragraph command.

Step 2 Click the Paragraph command.
Point to the down arrow button in the Line spacing drop-down list box in the Paragraph dialog box.

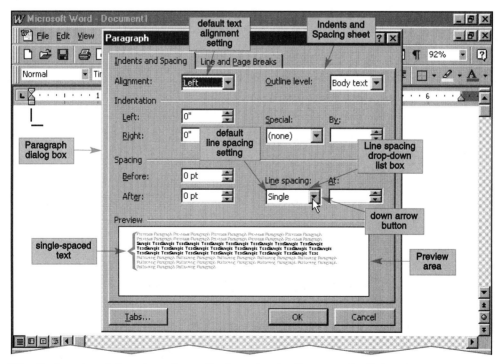

Figure 19

The Indents and Spacing sheet displays in the Paragraph dialog box. The Line spacing drop-down list box contains the highlighted default line spacing setting (Single), the Preview area contains a sample of single-spaced text, and the mouse pointer points to the down arrow button.

Step 3 Click the down arrow button.
Point to the Double setting in the Line spacing
drop-down list.

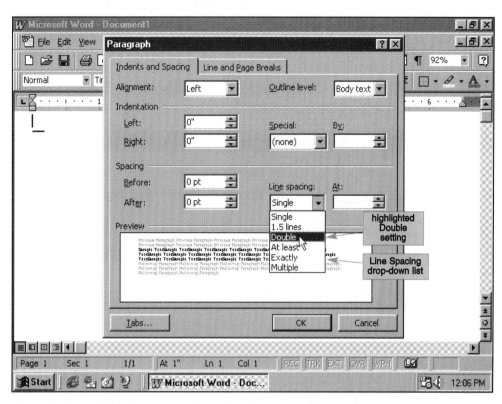

Figure 20

The Line spacing drop-down list displays, and the mouse pointer points to the
highlighted Double setting.

Step 4 Click the Double setting.
Point to the OK button in the Paragraph dialog box.

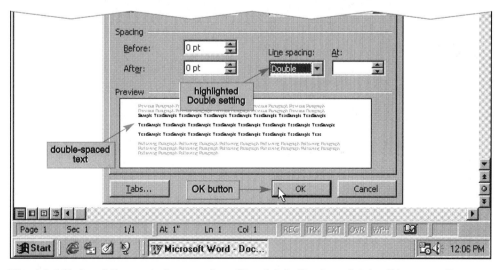

Figure 21

The highlighted line spacing setting (Double) displays in the Line spacing
drop-down list box, the Preview area contains a sample of double-spaced
text, and the mouse pointer points to the OK button.

Step 5   Click the OK button.

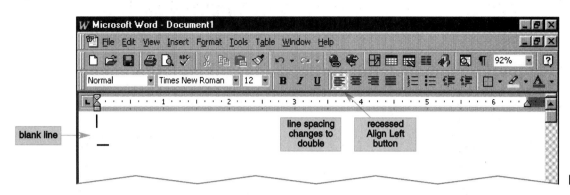

blank line

line spacing changes to double

recessed Align Left button

Figure 22

Line spacing is set to double, and a blank line displays between the insertion point and end mark in the text area to indicate the change to double spacing.

In Figure 19 on page 16, the Alignment drop-down list box contains the **default text justification setting** (Left). The next section, in which you will create the running head, explains this setting and text justification.

The Running Head (Header) and Text Justification

A **running head** prints at the top of each page of a document. It usually is inside the top margin and contains information relevant to the document, such as page number, date, or author's name. The MLA guidelines for a running head are:

1. Place the running head one-half inch down from the top of the page.
2. Place the author's last name and the page number in the running head. Number each page consecutively.
3. Display the running head flush with the right margin.

In Word terminology, a running head is called a **header**. The **default header setting** is one-half inch. Recall that the Header drop-down list box in the Page Setup dialog box shown in Figure 8 on page 11 contains the default header setting (0.5"). This default setting satisfies the MLA requirement that the running head display one-half inch from the top of the page.

Previously, you changed the font size for the research paper from 10 point to 12 point. However, this change does not apply to the text in the header. Therefore, you must change the font size of the header to 12 point before typing the text in the header.

Justification is the process of aligning text between the left and right margins. Left justification is the **default text justification**. **Left justification** causes the text to align with the left margin. The recessed Align Left button on the Formatting toolbar shown in Figure 22 indicates the default is left justification. Therefore, you must change the text justification to right justification to satisfy the MLA requirement that the running head be flush with the right margin.

Creating a Header

In the process of creating a header, Word switches from Normal view to Page Layout view. **Page Layout view** allows you to view headers and footnotes in a document. The following steps create the header for the research paper.

Step 1   Click View on the menu bar.
Point to the Header and Footer command on the
    View menu.

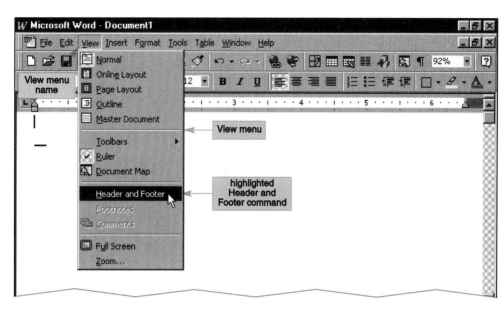

Figure 23

The View menu displays, and the mouse pointer points to the highlighted
Header and Footer command.

Step 2   Click the Header and Footer command.
Point to the Align Right button on the Formatting
    toolbar.

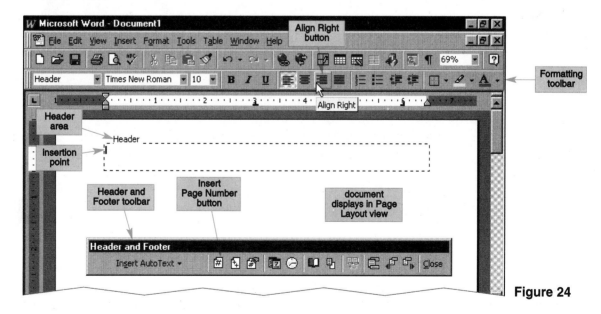

Figure 24

The document displays in Page Layout view, and the Header area and Header
and Footer toolbar display. The **Header area** contains the insertion point. The
Header and Footer toolbar contains the button to insert a page number in
the header. The mouse pointer points to the Align Right button on the
Formatting toolbar.

Step 3   Click the Align Right button.
Type **Forsythe** (author's last name) in the Header area.
Press the SPACEBAR.
Point to the Insert Page Number button on the
    Header and Footer toolbar.

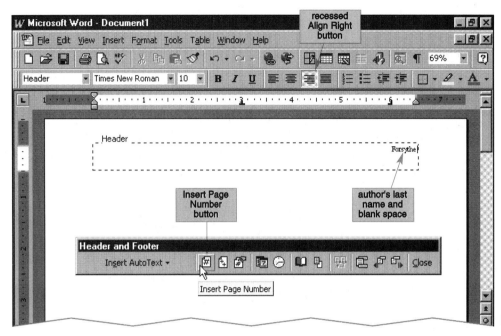

Figure 25

The Align Right button recesses, and the author's last name (Forsythe), a blank space, and the insertion point display right justified in the Header area. The mouse pointer points to the Insert Page Number button.

Step 4   Click the Insert Page Number button.
Point to a blank area to the left of the author's
    last name in the Header area.

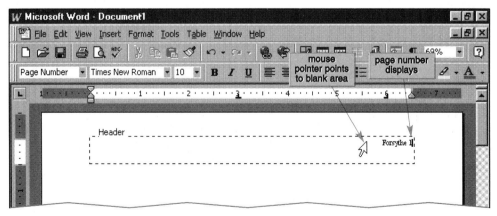

Figure 26

The page number (1) displays following the author's last name and blank space, and the mouse pointer points to the blank area to the left of the author's last name.

Step 5 Click the blank area to the left of the author's name.
Click the down arrow in the Font Size drop-down
list box.
Click the number 12 in the Font Size drop-down list.
Point to the Close button on the Header and
Footer toolbar.

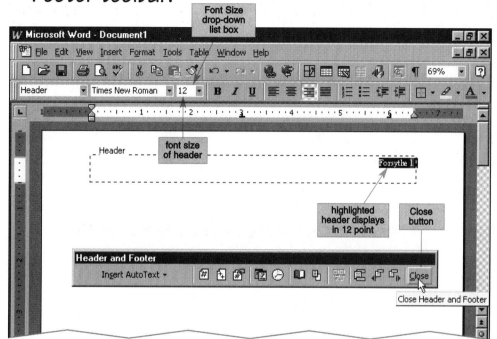

Figure 27

Word selects the text (author's last name, blank space, and page number) in
the Header area, the number 12 displays in the Font Size drop-down list box,
the font size of the header changes to 12 point, and the mouse pointer points
to the Close button on the Header and Footer toolbar.

Step 6 Click the Close button.

Word switches from Page Layout view to Normal view and removes the
Header area and Header and Footer toolbar.

The creation of the header is complete. Although the header does not display in the document
window in Normal view, you can **view the header** by clicking View on the menu bar and then clicking
the Page Layout command. After viewing the header, click View on the menu bar and then click the
Normal command to return to Normal view.

If you wish to **edit the header**, click View on the menu bar, and then click the Header and Footer
command to switch to Page Layout view and display the Header area and Header and Footer toolbar.
After editing, click the Close button on the Header and Footer toolbar to save the changes and return to
Normal view.

Typing the Body of the Research Paper

The **body** of the research paper consists of the text of the paper, excluding the Works Cited page. In Figure 1 on pages 2 and 3, the body consists of the first two pages of the research paper. The tasks involved in typing the body of the research paper include:

1. Typing your name and course information.
2. Centering the research paper title.
3. Indenting the first line of each paragraph.
4. Typing parenthetical citations and footnotes as needed.
5. Inserting tables as needed.
6. Saving the research paper on a disk.

As you will remember from word processing classes, you can easily correct errors as you type by pressing the BACKSPACE key to delete the incorrect character or characters and then typing the correct text.

Typing the Name and Course Information

Most scholarly papers include a title page. The MLA style, however, indicates a title page is not required when creating a research paper. Instead, you can type your full name, the professor's name, the course name and number, and the paper's due date on separate lines at the top of the first page. These lines should begin one inch from the top of the first page and display flush with the left margin.

Recall that the **default top margin** is 1 inch, and left justification is the **default text justification**. These settings conform to the MLA standards to begin the research paper one inch from the top of the first page and flush with the left margin. The following step enters the author's name and course information.

Step 1   Type **Steven Forsythe** and press the ENTER key.
Type **Professor Susan Kirkwood** and press the ENTER key.
Type **English Composition 101** and press the ENTER key.
Type **August 17, 2000** and press the ENTER key.

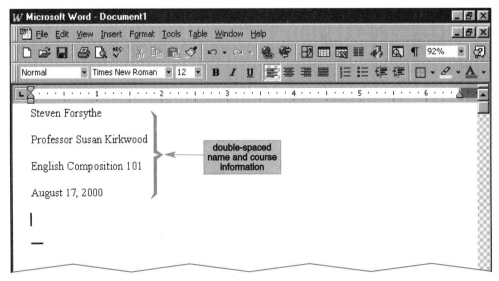

Figure 28

The entries for author name, professor name, course name and number, and paper due date are double-spaced and display on separate lines.

Entering the name and course information is complete. The four lines of information begin one inch from the top of the first page, display on separate lines, and are left justified and double-spaced.

You may have noticed that after typing the first four characters of the name of the month (Augu), the **AutoComplete feature** detected you were typing a month name and displayed a box containing the full month name (August) above the four characters. At this point, Word allows you to press the ENTER key to replace the four characters in the document (Augu) with the complete month name (August).

Centering the Research Paper Title

The MLA guidelines for the research paper state that the title of the paper should display below the name and course information and be centered between the left and right margins. As mentioned previously, left justification is the default text justification. To satisfy the MLA requirement, you will need to center the research paper title.

In Step 2 on page 24, you will type an incorrectly spelled word (Reserch) instead of the correctly spelled word (Research). This is done to illustrate the spell check feature in a later section. The following steps illustrate how to type and center the research paper title.

Step 1 **Point to the Center button on the Formatting toolbar.**

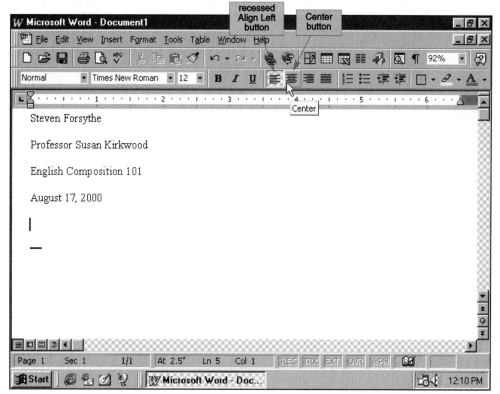

Figure 29

The mouse pointer points to the Center button, and the recessed Align Left button displays on the Formatting toolbar.

Step 2 Click the Center button.
Type **Locating Sources for a Reserch Paper** as the paper title.
Press the ENTER key.
Point to the Align Left button.

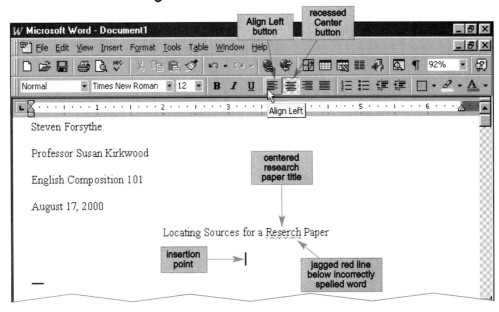

Figure 30

Word moves the insertion point to the center of the line and recesses the
Center button, the title is typed and displays centered between the left and
right margins, the insertion point displays centered on the line below the title,
and the mouse pointer points to the Align Left button. Although the color is
not visible in Figure 30, a **jagged red line** displays below the incorrectly
spelled word, Reserch, in the title.

Step 3 Click the Align Left button.

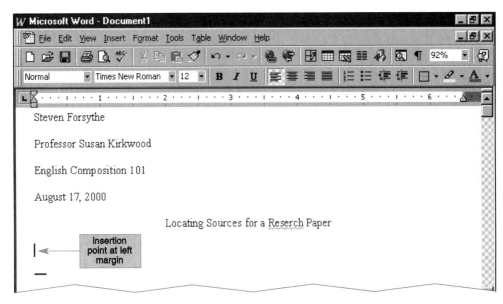

Figure 31

The insertion point moves to the left margin.

The research paper title displays centered on the line below the name and course information. A jagged red line displays below the incorrectly spelled word, Reserch, in the title. The following section will illustrate how to correct this misspelling.

Correcting Misspelled Words as You Type

In Step 2 on page 24, you typed the incorrectly spelled word, Reserch, in the research paper title, and a jagged red line displayed below the word to indicate the word was not in the **Word dictionary**.

To correct the incorrectly spelled word, you will right-click the word, Reserch, in the research paper title. Recall that **right-click** means press and release the right mouse button. The following steps replace the incorrectly spelled word, Reserch, with the correctly spelled word, Research.

Step 1   Right-click the word, Reserch, by pressing and releasing the right mouse button.
Point to the word, Research, on the shortcut menu.

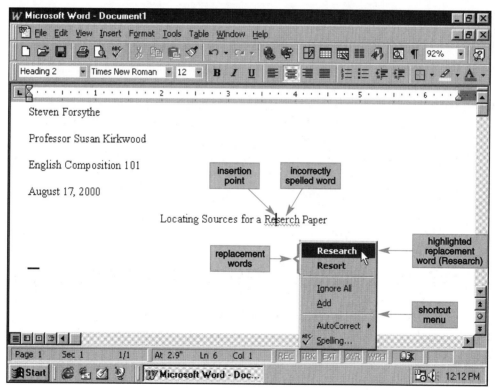

Figure 32

The insertion point is positioned in the word, Reserch, and a shortcut menu displays. A **shortcut menu** is a menu that contains commands for use with the object you right-click. In this instance, the shortcut menu contains two suggested replacement words for the incorrectly spelled word, Reserch. The mouse pointer points to the highlighted word, Research.

Step 2   Click the word, Research.
          Press the Page Down (PG DN) key on the keyboard
          to move the insertion point to the end of the
          document.

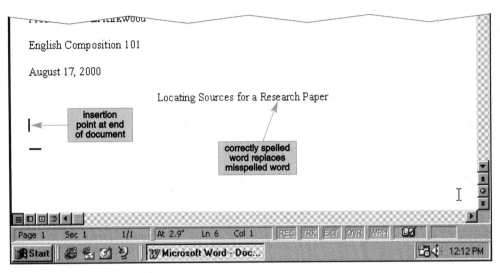

English Composition 101

August 17, 2000

Locating Sources for a Research Paper

insertion
point at end
of document

correctly spelled
word replaces
misspelled word

Page 1   Sec 1   1/1   At 2.9"   Ln 6   Col 1   REC TRK EXT OVR WPH

Start   Microsoft Word - Doc...   12:12 PM

Figure 33

Word replaces the misspelled word, Reserch, with the correctly spelled word,
Research, from the shortcut menu and moves the insertion point to the end of
the document.

    In addition to correcting misspelled words, the **AutoCorrect feature** automatically corrects
common typing, spelling, and grammatical errors as you type. For example, if you type teh, Word
automatically recognizes the misspelled word and replaces the word, teh, with the word, the, when you
press the SPACEBAR following the entry of the word. In addition, if you type a word incorrectly and
realize your mistake as you are typing, you can use the BACKSPACE key to delete the incorrect text and
then type the correct text.
    A jagged green line that displays below a word or words in a sentence indicates the **Grammar
Checker** has detected a sentence that is grammatically in error. To fix the problem, right-click the
underlined word in the sentence to display a shortcut menu containing suggestions.
    Although you should correct errors as you type, you may also spell check the entire document after
typing, proofreading, and revising the research paper. The section titled, Using the Office Assistant to
Obtain Help, starting on page 73 contains a help topic that explains how to spell check an entire
document.

Indenting a Paragraph

When typing paragraphs, the MLA guidelines indicate you should indent the first line of every paragraph
in the research paper one-half inch from the left margin. In Word, the default tabs are set at half-inch
intervals, so pressing the TAB key before typing the first line moves the insertion point one-half inch
toward the right margin, causing the indentation of the first line of the paragraph. The step on the next
page indents and types the first paragraph of the research paper.

Step 1 Press the TAB key.
        Type the first paragraph of the research paper as
            shown in Figure 34.
        Press the ENTER key.
        Correct the misspelled words, as you type and
            press the Page Down (PG DN) key to move the
            insertion point to the end of the document.

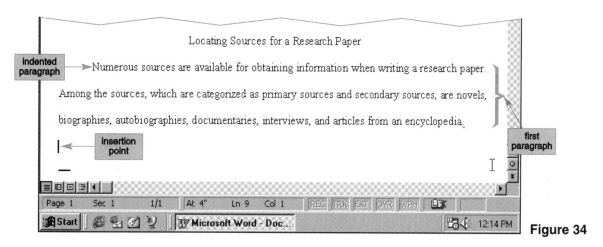

Figure 34

The first paragraph of the research paper is typed, the first line of the paragraph is indented, one-half inch from the left margin, and the insertion point displays on the blank line following the paragraph.

The first paragraph in the research paper displays below the centered research paper title. The first line of the paragraph is indented, and the insertion point displays at the left margin on the blank line below the paragraph.

Parenthetical Citations

The MLA guidelines for documenting references within a research paper are to place a parenthetical citation in the body of the research paper and a corresponding entry in the Works Cited list. A **parenthetical citation** indicates you have incorporated the ideas, words, or facts of another individual into your research paper. The corresponding reference in the Works Cited list contains the details about the source of the information (author's name, book or article title, publisher, and so on).

When typing a parenthetical citation, follow these MLA guidelines:

1. Insert parentheses around each parenthetical citation.
2. Include the author's last name, a blank space, and a page or date reference.
3. If the citation references multiple pages, the page reference should consist of the beginning page number, a hyphen (-), and the ending page number.

Figure 35 on the next page contains the first two paragraphs on the first page of the research paper shown in Figure 1 on pages 2 and 3, and the top of the Works Cited page. A parenthetical citation containing the author's last name and page reference (Williams 57) displays at the end of the second paragraph.

The Works Cited page contains a reference for each parenthetical citation in the research paper. The third reference on the Works Cited page (Williams, Susan. "Locating and Evaluating Primary and Secondary Sources." <u>Writer's Monthly</u> 17 Oct. 1998: 57.) corresponds to the (Williams 57) citation in the research paper. The citation references a magazine article.

Forsythe 1

Steven Forsythe

Professor Susan Kirkwood

English Composition 101

August 17, 2000

Locating Sources for a Research Paper

Numerous sources are available for obtaining information when writing a research paper.

Among the sources, which are categorized as primary sources and secondary sources, are novels,

biographies, autobiographies, documentaries, interviews, and articles from an encyclopedia.

A primary source is an original work created by an author. As such, it is more accurate

than a secondary source. An autobiography, an interview you conduct, a novel, a play, or a

speech is a primary source. A secondary source is an interpretation of a primary source. As such,

it can be biased and inaccurate. A review, a biography, a documentary, or an article from an

encyclopedia is a secondary source (Williams 57). ← parenthetical citation

Finding useful information for a research paper is a .... skill. Over time, a good

---

Forsythe 3

Works Cited

Anderson, Peter. "Popular Internet Resources." Internet Research Journal 4 (1999). 12 Mar. 2000

    <http://www.irj.com>.

Howard, Stanley. Creating a Working Bibliography. Fort Lauderdale: Literary Press, 1999.

reference → Williams, Susan. "Locating and Evaluating Primary and Secondary Sources." Writer's Monthly

    17 Oct. 1998: 57.

Figure 35

For examples of parenthetical citations that conform to the MLA guidelines, ask your teacher, consult the *MLA Handbook for Writers of Research Papers* written by Joseph Gibaldi, or visit our Web site (www.stevenspress.com).

Typing the First Parenthetical Citation

When typing a parenthetical citation, the MLA guidelines indicate you should place parentheses around the citation and include the author's last name, a blank space, and a page or date reference. Perform the following step to type the second paragraph of the research paper and the first parenthetical citation.

Step 1 Press the TAB key.
Type the second paragraph of the research paper as shown in Figure 36.
Press the ENTER key.

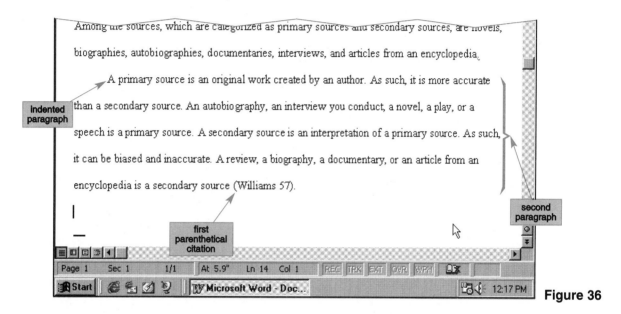

Figure 36

The second paragraph of the research paper is typed, the first line of the paragraph is indented, and the last sentence in the paragraph contains the (Williams 57) citation.

Saving a Document

After completing a substantial portion of a document, you should save the document on disk to prevent its accidental loss. Before you save the document, you must decide on a file name for it. A **file name** uniquely identifies a document on a disk, can consist of up to 255 characters, and should be descriptive of the document's contents. A descriptive but brief file name is preferable.

Although a file name can consist of blank spaces, uppercase characters, and lowercase characters, the following characters cannot be used: asterisk (*), backslash (\), colon (:), greater than symbol (>), less than symbol (<), question mark (?), quotation mark ("), semicolon (;), slash (/), and vertical bar (|). In addition, you cannot use the following system file names as file names: COM, AUX, COM1, COM2, COM3, COM4, LPT1, LPT2, LPT3, PRN, or NUL.

Most documents stored on disk also have a **file extension** that identifies the application program used to create the file. All documents you create using Microsoft Word have the .doc file extension.

Saving the Research Paper

To prevent the accidental loss of the research paper, you should give your document an appropriate file name and save it on a 3½" floppy disk in drive A. In this book, you will use the research paper title (Locating Sources for a Research Paper) as the file name. Because this is the first time you have saved the document, you will need a blank, formatted floppy disk. To identify the floppy disk, write the words, Research Papers, on the paper label attached to the outside of the disk.

The **default drive setting** for storing files is drive C, and the **default folder setting** for storing files is the My Documents folder. To save the document on a floppy disk in drive A, you must change the default drive and default folder settings. The following steps save the document containing the research paper on a floppy disk in drive A using Locating Sources for a Research Paper as the file name.

Step 1   Insert a formatted floppy disk in drive A.

Step 2   Point to the Save button on the Standard toolbar.

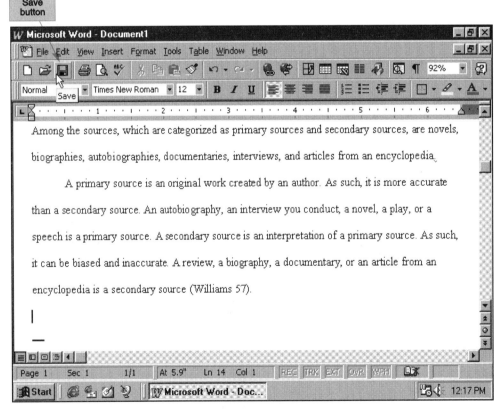

Figure 37

The mouse pointer points to the Save button.

Step 3   Click the Save button.

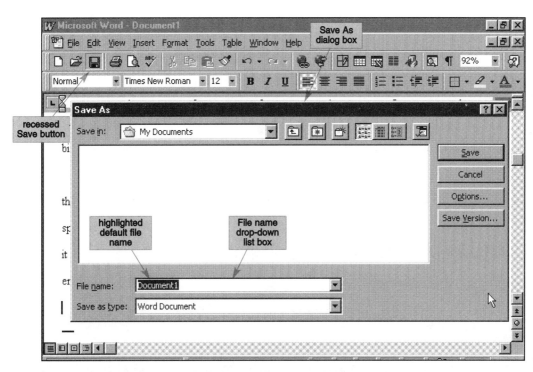

Figure 38

Word recesses the Save button and opens the Save As dialog box. The highlighted default file name (Document1) or a previously used file name displays in the File name drop-down list box.

Step 4 Type **Locating Sources for a Research Paper** in the File name drop-down list box.
Point to the down arrow button in the Save in drop-down list box.

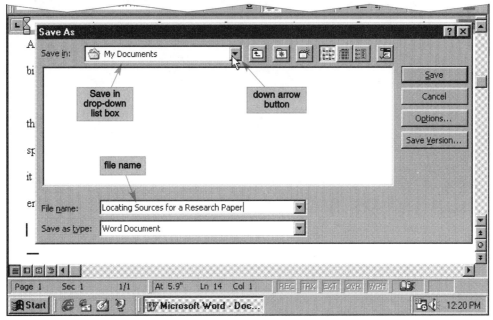

Figure 39

The Locating Sources for a Research Paper file name displays in the File name drop-down list box, and the mouse pointer points to the down arrow button in the Save in drop-down list box.

Step 5   Click the down arrow button.
Point to the 3½ Floppy (A:) drive name in the Save in drop-down list.

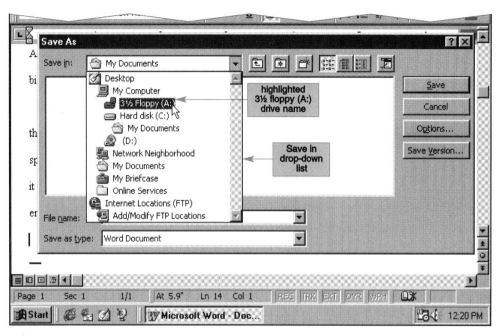

Figure 40

The Save in drop-down list opens, and the mouse pointer points to the highlighted 3½ Floppy (A:) drive name.

Step 6   Click the 3½ Floppy (A:) drive name.
Point to the Save button in the Save As dialog box.

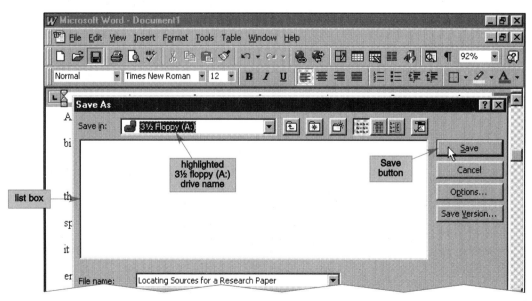

Figure 41

The Save in drop-down list closes, the highlighted 3½ Floppy (A:) drive name displays in the Save in drop-down list box, and the mouse pointer points to the Save button. If there are files on the floppy disk in drive A, a list of their file names displays in the list box.

Step 7 Click the Save button.

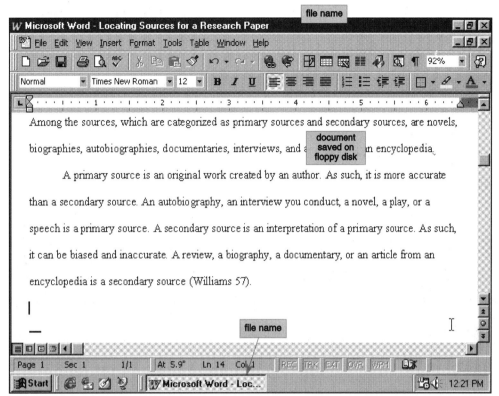

Figure 42

The Save As dialog box closes, Word saves the document on the floppy disk
in drive A using the Locating Sources for a Research Paper.doc file name,
and the new file name displays in the window title and on the taskbar button.

After saving the document for the first time, you should continue to save the document periodically to avoid losing information. Click the Save button on the Standard toolbar to save the document again using the same file name.

Footnotes

A **footnote** is an explanatory note that displays at the bottom of a page, and an **endnote** is an explanatory note that displays at the end of the document. Although the MLA style suggests the use of parenthetical citations instead of footnotes or endnotes, some of the humanities disciplines (art, history, music, religion, theology, and history) continue to use footnotes or endnotes to document their sources.

In this book, we included both parenthetical citations and footnotes in the same research paper to illustrate their uses. Check with your teacher to determine whether you should use parenthetical citations, footnotes and endnotes, or a combination of both in your research paper.

If a section of text in the research paper needs further explanation and you wish to use footnotes in the research paper, place a footnote number following the text in the body of the research paper and place the footnote at the bottom of the page. Figure 43 on the next page illustrates the bottom of page one of the research paper shown in Figure 1 on pages 2 and 3.

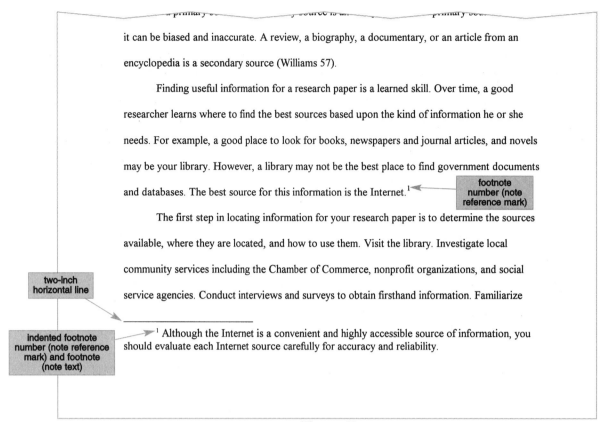

Figure 43

A footnote number, or **superscript** (raised number 1), follows the last sentence in the third paragraph. The same superscript number also precedes the footnote at the bottom of the page. The footnote number 1 associates the sentence in the research paper with the footnote at the bottom of the page. When placing a footnote in a research paper, follow these MLA guidelines:

1. Separate all footnotes at the bottom of the page from the text on the page with a two-inch horizontal line.
2. Indent the first line of each footnote one half-inch from the left margin.
3. Single-space each footnote, and double-space between footnotes.
4. Use the same font and font size as the text of the research paper.

In Word terminology, a footnote consists of two parts: the **note reference mark** (superscripted footnote number) and the **note text** (footnote). By default, Word places the appropriate note reference mark (starting with the number 1) following the text that needs further explanation in the research paper, draws a two-inch horizontal line at the appropriate position at the bottom of the page, and displays the note text below the horizontal line. Word automatically renumbers the note reference marks in a document if you add, delete, or move a note.

Previously in this book, you changed the font size to 12 point and line spacing to double spacing. Because this change does not affect footnotes, you must change the font size to 12 point before you type a footnote. If more than one footnote displays at the bottom of a page, you should double-space between the footnotes.

Creating a Footnote

When you create the first footnote in the research paper, Word assigns the appropriate note reference mark (1) to the footnote and displays a two-inch separator line at the bottom of the page. In addition, Word displays the note reference mark following the text that needs a further explanation in the body of the research paper and displays the same note reference mark preceding the note text at the bottom of the page. You then type the note text following the note reference mark at the bottom of the page.

Perform the following steps to type the third paragraph and create a footnote at the end of the paragraph.

Step 1 Press the TAB key.

Type the third paragraph of the research paper as shown in Figure 44. DO NOT press the ENTER key.

Correct misspelled words as you type, and press the Page Down (PG DN) key to move the insertion point to the end of the document.

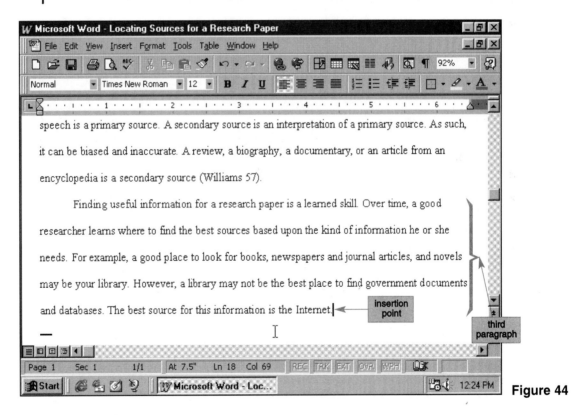

Figure 44

The third paragraph of the research paper is typed, and the insertion point displays following the last sentence in the paragraph.

Step 2 Click Insert on the menu bar.
Point to the Footnote command on the Insert menu.

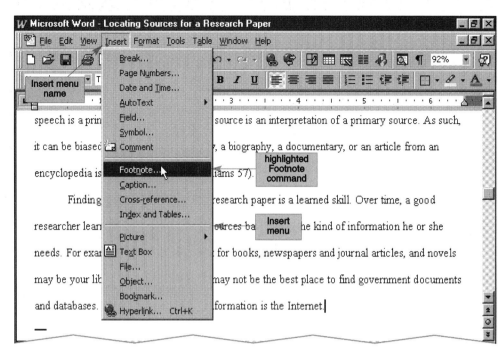

Figure 45

The Insert menu displays, and the mouse points to the highlighted Footnote command.

Step 3 Click the Footnote command.
Point to the OK button in the Footnote and
Endnote dialog box.

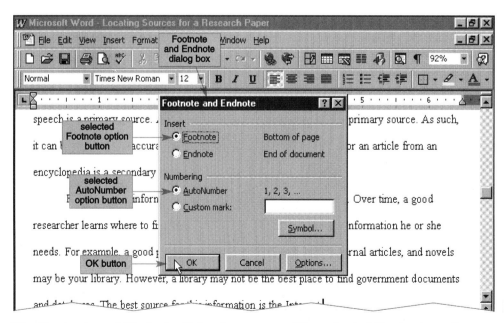

Figure 46

The Footnote and Endnote dialog box opens. The selected Footnote option button indicates Word will insert a footnote in the research paper, and the selected AutoNumber option button indicates Word will automatically number the footnote.

Step 4 Click the OK button.

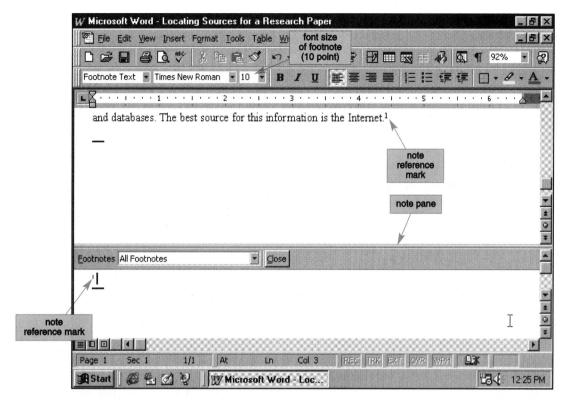

Figure 47

A note reference mark (superscript 1) displays at the end of the third paragraph, the number 10 displays in the Font Size drop-down list box on the Formatting toolbar, and the note pane displays in the lower section of the window. The **note pane** contains a note reference mark (superscript 1), a blank space, and the insertion point.

Step 5 Press the HOME key to move the insertion point to the left of the note reference mark in the note pane. Press the TAB key to indent the footnote. Press the END key to move the insertion point to the right of the reference mark.

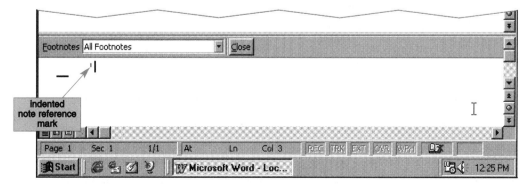

Figure 48

Word indents the note reference mark one-half inch. The insertion point is located following the note reference mark and blank space.

Step 6   Click the down arrow button in the Font Size drop-down
         list box.
         Click 12 in the Font Size drop-down list.

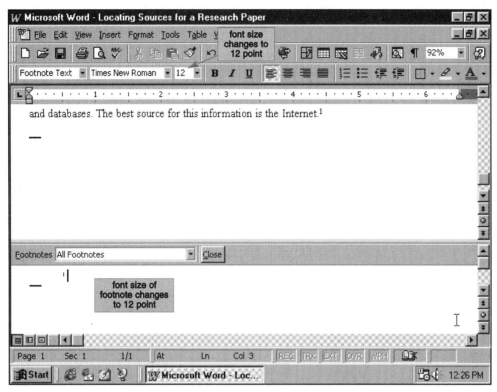

Figure 49

The font size in the note pane changes to 12 point and the number 12 displays
in the Font Size drop-down list box.

Step 7   Type the note text as shown in Figure 50.
         Correct misspelled words as you type, and press
            the Page Down (Pg Dn) key to move the insertion
            point to the end of the note text.
         Point to the Close button in the note pane.

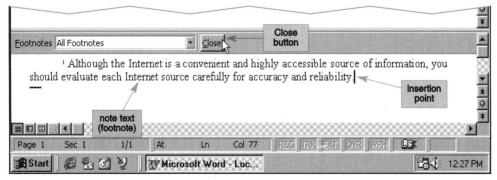

Figure 50

The note text is typed, and the insertion point displays at the end of the
note text. The mouse pointer points to the Close button.

Step 8   Click the Close button.
Press the ENTER key to terminate the entry of the footnote.

> The note pane closes, and the note reference mark displays in the research paper.

The creation of the footnote is complete. Although the footnote does not display in the text area in Normal view, you can **view the footnote** at any time by pointing to the note reference mark.

If you wish to **edit the footnote**, click View on the menu bar and click the Footnotes command, or double-click the note reference mark in the body of the research paper to display the note pane. When you have finished editing the footnote, click the Close button in the note pane.

Viewing an Automatic Page Break

A **page break** is the point at which one page ends and another page begins. When you type text into a document and the text will not fit on a single page, Word inserts an **automatic page break** in the document, adds a new page to the document, and displays the overflow of text on the new page.

In Normal view, an automatic page break displays as a single dotted horizontal line. As you type the fourth paragraph in the research paper, Word will insert an automatic page break in the document. Perform the following step to type the fourth paragraph, insert an automatic page break, and create a new page in the research paper.

Step 1   Press the TAB key, type the fourth paragraph of the research paper as shown in Figure 51, and press the ENTER key.
Correct misspelled words as you type, and press the Page Down (PG DN) key to move the insertion point to the end of the document.

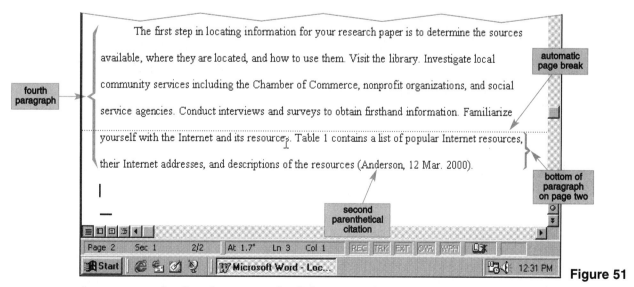

Figure 51

As you type the fourth paragraph of the research paper, Word inserts an automatic page break in the document, creates a second page, and displays the end of the fourth paragraph at the top of the second page. The last sentence in the paragraph contains the citation (Anderson, 12 Mar. 2000).

Tables

Although not every research paper will contain a table, the MLA guidelines include instructions for their use in a research paper. A **table** is an orderly arrangement of data in rows and columns. A **row** is a series of horizontal cells, and a **column** is a series of vertical cells. The horizontal lines of the rows and the vertical lines of the columns divide the table into rectangular areas called **cells**. A cell may contain text, numbers, or graphic images. Figure 52 contains the table from the research paper shown in Figure 1 on pages 2 and 3.

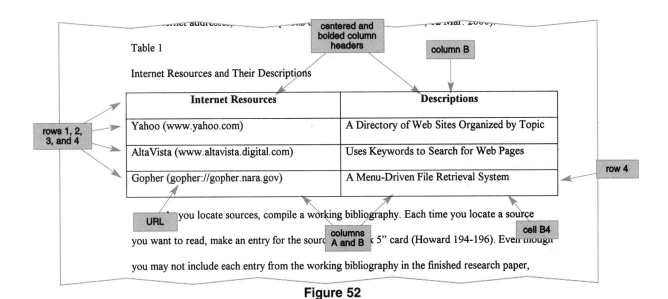

Figure 52

You can reference each cell in the table if you know its row number and column letter. Rows are labeled from top to bottom starting with the number 1. Columns are labeled from left to right starting with the letter A. The table in Figure 52 consists of two columns and four rows. You can locate a cell in a table using its **cell address**. For example, the cell address of the cell at the intersection of the second column (B) and the fourth row (4) is cell B4.

In the table shown in Figure 52, each cell in the first row (cells A1 and B1) contains a column header. A **column header** identifies the text that displays in the remaining cells in that column. The column headers in the table display in bold type and are centered within their cells.

The cells below the column headers contain text. Some cells (cells A2, A3, and A4) contain Uniform Resource Locators (URLs) enclosed in parentheses. A URL is a link to a Web page on the Internet.

When using a table in a research paper, follow the MLA guidelines below:

1. Place the table as close as possible to the text that references the table.
2. Add a label to the table. A **label** consists of the word, Table, and an Arabic numeral (Table 1), and displays flush left on a separate line above the table.
3. Add a caption to the table. A **caption** displays flush left on a separate line between the label and table. The first letter of each word is capitalized (initial caps).
4. If you took the data in the table from another source, place the source of the table below the table. The source consists of the word, Source, a colon (:), and the source of the information in the table.

The following sections illustrate how to insert a table in a research paper.

Inserting an Empty Table

First, insert an empty table in the research paper. When you insert an empty table, you must specify the number of rows and columns it will contain. The table in Figure 52, referred to as a 4x2 table, consists of four rows and two columns. In the following steps, you will type the table label and table caption, and insert an empty 4x2 table in the research paper.

Step 1 Type **Table 1** as the label for the table and press the ENTER key.
Type **Internet Resources and Their Descriptions** as the table caption and press the ENTER key.
Point to the Insert Table button on the Standard toolbar.

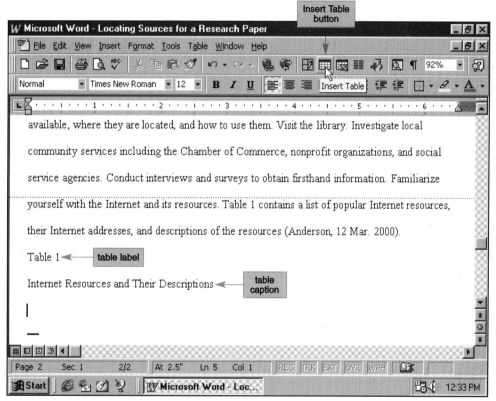

Figure 53

The label and caption display in the research paper, and the mouse pointer points to the Insert Table button.

Step 2 Click the Insert Table button.
Point to the fourth cell in the second column as
shown in Figure 54.

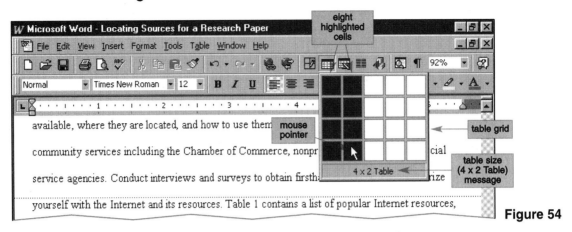

Figure 54

A **table grid** displays, the mouse pointer points to the fourth cell in the
second column of the table grid, Word highlights the first two columns and
first four rows (eight cells) in the table grid, and the words, 4 x 2 Table,
display at the bottom of the table grid.

Step 3 Click the fourth cell in the second column.
Click the down scroll arrow on the vertical scroll bar
six times to view the entire table.

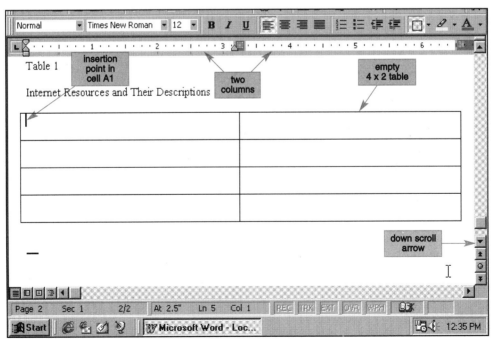

Figure 55

  Word inserts an empty 4 x 2 table in the research paper and moves the
insertion point to cell A1. Two columns display on the horizontal ruler to
indicate the table has two columns.

Entering Text in the Table

Next, type the contents of the table cells. Recall from Figure 52 on page 40 that row 1 of the table contains the column headers and rows 2, 3, and 4 contain the text of the table.

To move the insertion point within a table, use the TAB key. For example, if the insertion point is in cell A1 and you wish to move the insertion point to cell B1, press the TAB key. If the insertion point is located in the rightmost cell of a row, pressing the TAB key will move the insertion point to the first cell in the next row. In the following steps, you will enter the column headers in row one and text in rows two, three, and four.

Step 1   Verify the insertion point is located in cell A1.
Click the Center button on the Formatting toolbar.
Click the Bold button on the Formatting toolbar.
Type **Internet Resources** in cell A1.
Press the TAB key.
Click the Center button on the Formatting toolbar.
Click the Bold button on the Formatting toolbar.
Type **Descriptions** in cell B1.
Press the TAB key.

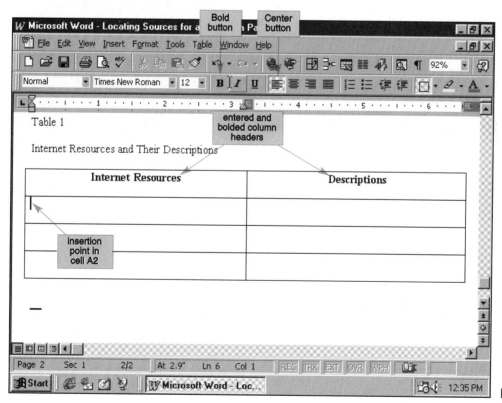

Figure 56

The bold and centered column headers display in cells A1 and B1, and the insertion point is located in cell A2.

Step 2 Type **Yahoo (www.yahoo.com)** in cell A2.
Press the TAB key and type **A Directory of Web Sites Organized by Topic** in cell B2.
Press the TAB key and type **AltaVista (www.altavista.digital.com)** in cell A3.
Press the TAB key and type **Uses Keywords to Search for Web Pages** in cell B3.
Press the TAB key and type **Gopher (gopher://gopher.nara.gov)** in cell A4.
Press the TAB key and type **A Menu-Driven File Retrieval System** in cell B4.
Correct misspelled words as you type.

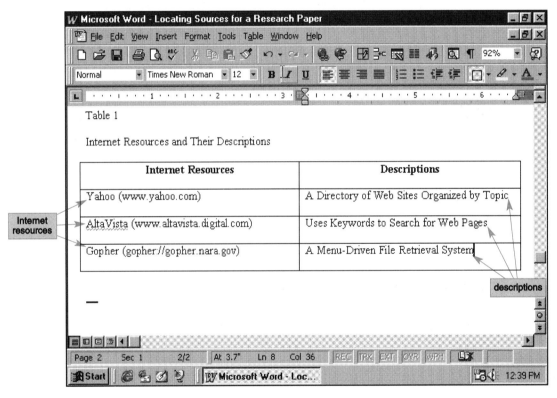

Figure 57

The remainder of the text in the table is typed, and the table is spell checked.

If you make a mistake while typing text in a cell, you can use the DELETE key and BACKSPACE key to correct the text. Pressing the DELETE key removes the character to the right of the insertion point, and pressing the BACKSPACE key removes the character to the left of the insertion point. If you notice a mistake in a cell that does not contain the insertion point, click the cell to move the insertion point into it, and then use the DELETE key or BACKSPACE key to correct the text.

If you type text in a table cell and the text exceeds the width of the cell, the height of the cell is increased to accommodate the text, and text that does not fit on the first line in the cell moves to a second line in the cell. If this happens, you should select the entire table and change the line spacing to single spacing using the Paragraph command on the Format menu.

Inserting a Blank Line Before a Paragraph

When you move the insertion point from its location in the table to the blank line below the table, Word does not maintain the double spacing of the research paper. To maintain the double spacing of the research paper, insert a blank line by holding down the CTRL key and pressing the 0 (zero) key, and then type the paragraph below the table. If you type a second paragraph below the table, you must hold down the CTRL key and press the 0 (zero) key again before typing the second paragraph to remove the extra blank line that displays below the first paragraph. Perform the following steps to insert a blank line and cause the document to look double-spaced.

Step 1 Click the blank line below the table to move the insertion point to the blank line.

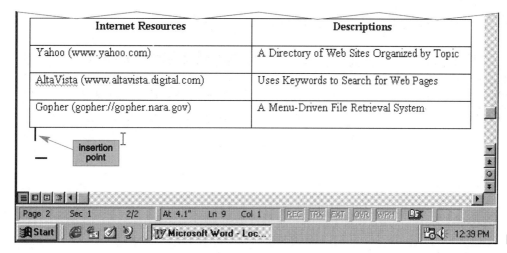

Figure 58

The insertion point displays at the beginning of the blank line below the table.

Step 2 Hold down the CTRL key and press the 0 (zero) key.

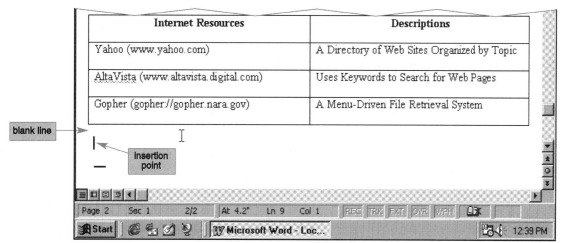

Figure 59

Word inserts a blank line, and the insertion point displays at the beginning of the second blank line below the table.

Typing the Remaining Two Paragraphs

In the following steps, you type the last two paragraphs of the research paper.

Step 1 Press the tab key.
Type the next paragraph of the research paper as shown in Figure 60.
Press the ENTER key.
Correct misspelled words, and press the Page Down (pg dn) key to move the insertion point to the end of the document.

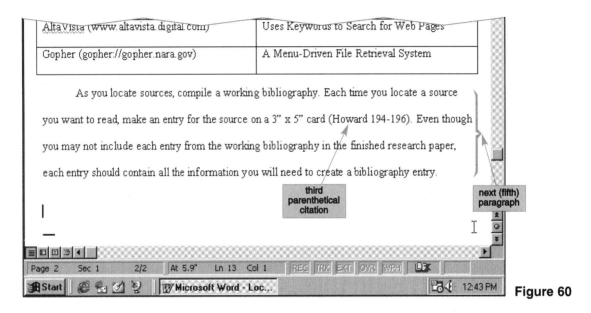

| AltaVista (www.altavista.digital.com) | Uses Keywords to Search for Web Pages |
| Gopher (gopher://gopher.nara.gov) | A Menu-Driven File Retrieval System |

As you locate sources, compile a working bibliography. Each time you locate a source you want to read, make an entry for the source on a 3" x 5" card (Howard 194-196). Even though you may not include each entry from the working bibliography in the finished research paper, each entry should contain all the information you will need to create a bibliography entry.

third parenthetical citation

next (fifth) paragraph

Page 2   Sec 1   2/2   At 5.9"   Ln 13   Col 1   REC TRK EXT OVR WPH

Start   Microsoft Word - Loc...   12:43 PM

Figure 60

The next paragraph of the research paper is typed. The second sentence in the paragraph contains a parenthetical citation (Howard 194-196).

Step 2 Hold down the CTRL key and press the 0 (zero) key.
Press the TAB key.
Type the last paragraph of the research paper as shown in Figure 61.
Press the ENTER key.
Correct misspelled words, and press the Page Down (PG DN) key to move the insertion point to the end of the document.

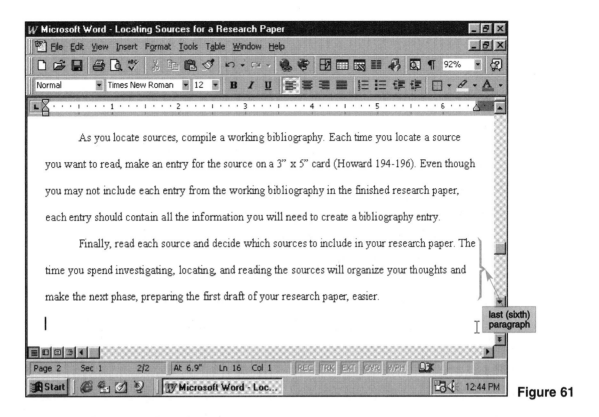

As you locate sources, compile a working bibliography. Each time you locate a source you want to read, make an entry for the source on a 3" x 5" card (Howard 194-196). Even though you may not include each entry from the working bibliography in the finished research paper, each entry should contain all the information you will need to create a bibliography entry.

Finally, read each source and decide which sources to include in your research paper. The time you spend investigating, locating, and reading the sources will organize your thoughts and make the next phase, preparing the first draft of your research paper, easier.

last (sixth) paragraph

Figure 61

The last paragraph of the research paper is typed.

This completes the entry of the body of the research paper. The next step in completing the research paper is to create the Works Cited list.

The Works Cited List

As mentioned previously, a parenthetical citation indicates to the reader that you have incorporated the ideas, words, or facts of another individual into your research paper. Each parenthetical citation that references a magazine article, book, newspaper article, the Internet, or other source used in the preparation of the research paper should have a corresponding reference in the Works Cited list. Each reference should contain the details about the source of the information referred to by the parenthetical citation. Follow the MLA guidelines described below to create the Works Cited list.

1. The Works Cited list should appear at the end of the research paper on a separate page. A header should appear on the Works Cited page that continues the numbering of the pages, and the text on the page should be double-spaced.
2. The centered title, Works Cited, should display one inch from the top of the paper on the first line of the page.
3. The first line of each reference should align with the left margin, and subsequent lines should begin one-half inch from the left margin.
4. The references should be in alphabetical order based on the author's last name.

Figure 62 on the next page illustrates the completed Works Cited page containing the three references for the three parenthetical citations in the research paper shown in Figure 1 on pages 2 and 3.

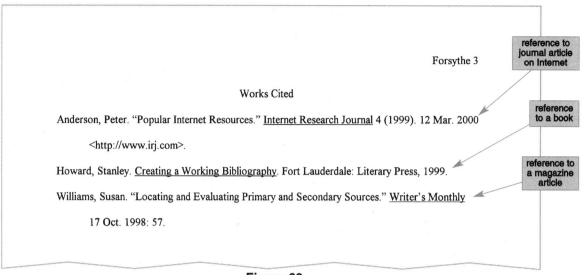

Figure 62

The first reference is to a journal article on the Internet, the second reference is to a book, and the third reference is to a magazine article. For more information about the MLA guidelines for composing references, ask your teacher, consult the *MLA Handbook for Writers of Research Papers* written by Joseph Gibaldi, or visit our Web site (www.stevenspress.com).

The following sections illustrate how to create the Works Cited list.

Inserting a Manual Page Break

Recall that a page break is the point at which one page ends and another page begins. Unlike the automatic page break that Word inserts in a document when you type text that will not fit on a single page, a **manual page break** is a page break you purposely insert into the research paper.

You create the page to contain the Works Cited list by inserting a manual page break into the research paper. In Normal view, a manual page break displays as a horizontal dotted line with the words, Page Break, centered on the dotted line. The following steps insert a manual page break in the research paper.

Step 1   Click Insert on the menu bar.
           Point to the Break command on the Insert menu.

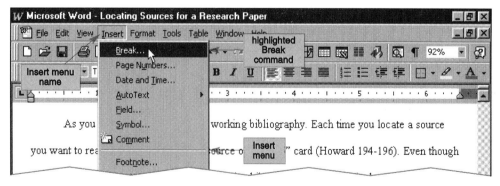

Figure 63

The Insert menu displays, and the mouse pointer points to the highlighted Break command.

Step 2 Click the Break command.
Point to the OK button in the Break dialog box.

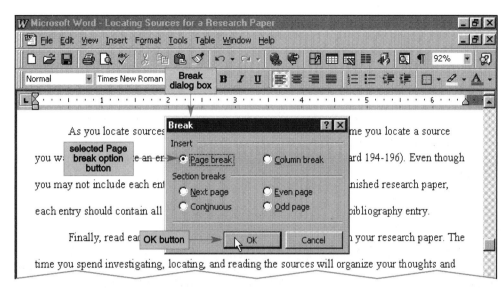

Figure 64

The selected Page break option button displays in the Break dialog box. The mouse pointer points to the OK button.

Step 3 Click the OK button.

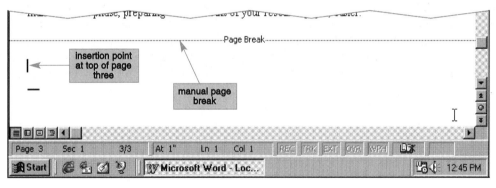

Figure 65

Word inserts a manual page break and creates a new (third) page. The insertion point displays at the top of the new page.

If you need to **remove a manual page break** from a document, highlight the manual page break by double-clicking the manual page break (horizontal dotted line), right-click the highlighted page break, and click the Cut command on the shortcut menu.

Centering the Works Cited Title

The procedure to center the Works Cited title is identical to the procedure used to center the research paper title (see Figures 29 through 31 on pages 23 and 24). In the following step, you will center and type the Works Cited title.

Step 1
Click the Center button on the Formatting toolbar.
Type **Works Cited** as the title.
Press the ENTER key.
Click the Align Left button on the Formatting toolbar.

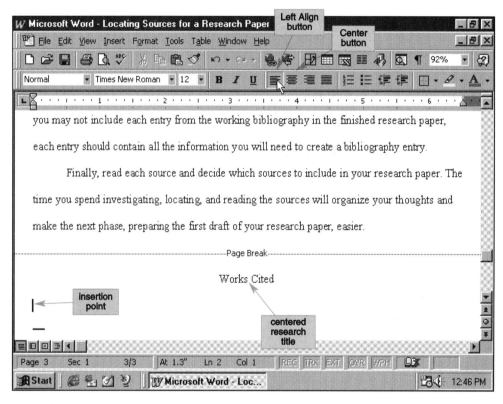

Figure 66

The Works Cited title displays centered between the left and right margins, and the insertion point moves to the left margin on the line below the title.

The centered Works Cited title displays at the top of page three.

Selecting Text

Many times when you work with text, you need to select a word, sentence, line, or paragraph. In Figures 26 and 27 on pages 20 and 21, you selected the header information by clicking the blank area to the left of the header. After typing the references on the Works Cited page, you will have to underline various parts of the references and sort the references by each author's last name. To accomplish this, you have to be able to select text. The table below summarizes various methods to select text.

TO SELECT	ACTION TO BE PERFORMED
A word	Double-click the word.
A sentence	Hold down the CTRL key and then click anywhere in the sentence.
A paragraph	Triple-click anywhere in the paragraph.
A line of text	Point to the left margin to change the pointer to a right-pointing white arrow, point to the left of the line, and click.
Several lines of text	Point to the left margin to change the pointer to a right-pointing white arrow, point to the left of the line, and drag the pointer up or down the left margin.
Multiple paragraphs	Point to the left margin to change the pointer to a right-pointing white arrow, point to the left of a paragraph, and drag the pointer up or down the left margin.

Table 1

Typing the References

Next, type a reference for each parenthetical citation in the research paper. Recall that the MLA guidelines require that the first line of each reference align with the left margin, and subsequent lines begin one-half inch from the left margin. In Word terminology, this is called a **hanging indent.**

To create a hanging indent, drag the Hanging Indent button on the ruler to the right along the ruler until the button rests on the .5-inch marker. Recall that **drag** means point to an object, hold down the left mouse button, move the object to the desired location, and release the left mouse button.

After creating a hanging indent, type each reference. Note that the third reference in the Works Cited list (see Figure 62 on page 48) contains a Uniform Resource Locator (URL) enclosed in angle brackets (<http://www.irj.com>). The URL is a link to a Web page on the Internet. If the link displays in underlined blue text, clicking the link starts the Web browser program on the computer, searches the Internet for the Web page associated with the link, and displays the Web page in a separate Web browser window.

The MLA guidelines for URLs enclose the reference to the URL in angle brackets. As a result, the link does not display in underlined blue text, and you cannot click the link to display the associated Web page. To satisfy this MLA guideline, type the URL (http://www.irj.com) followed by a period, move the insertion point to the left of the first character in the URL, click the LEFT ANGLE BRACKET key (<), move the insertion point to the right of the last character in the URL, and click the RIGHT ANGLE BRACKET key (>).

After typing the references, you will use the Underline button on the Formatting toolbar to underline titles of publications in the references. In the steps on the following three pages, you will create a hanging indent and type the three references in the Works Cited list.

Step 1 Point to the Hanging Indent button on the horizontal ruler.

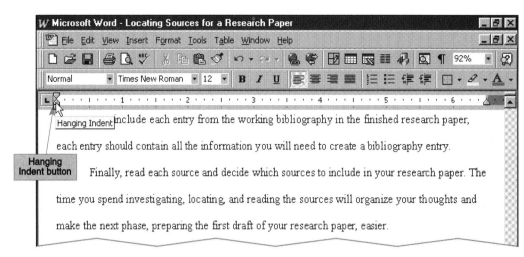

Figure 67

A ScreenTip containing the words, Hanging Indent, displays.

Step 2 Drag the Hanging Indent button to the .5-inch marker on the ruler by holding down the left mouse button, moving the button to the .5-inch marker on the ruler, and releasing the left mouse button.

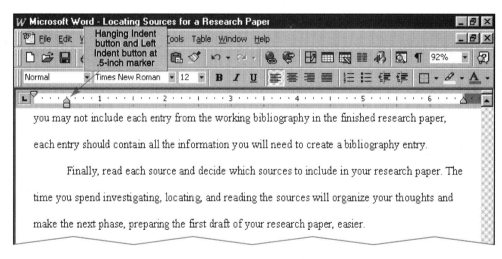

Figure 68

When you hold down the left mouse button, a dotted vertical line displays below the Hanging Indent button. When you drag the Hanging Indent button, the Hanging Indent button and the button below the Hanging Indent button (Left Indent button) move to the right along the ruler. When you release the left mouse button, the two buttons display at the .5-inch marker on the ruler.

Step 3 Type the three references (press the ENTER key after typing each reference) as shown in Figure 69. When you type the second reference, type **http://www.irj.com** followed by a period, move the insertion point to the left of the first character (h), and press the LEFT ANGLE BRACKET key (<). Then, move the insertion point to the right of the last character (m), press the RIGHT ANGLE BRACKET key (>), move the insertion point to the right of the period, and press the ENTER key.

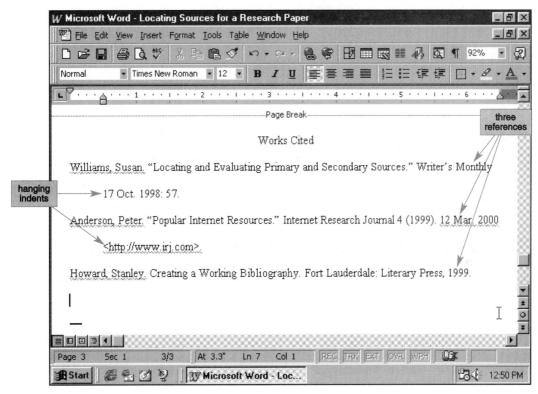

Figure 69

The three references are typed, the first line of each reference aligns with the left margin, and subsequent lines display one-half inch from the left margin. The second reference contains a link to a Web page on the Internet.

Step 4   Select the text, Writer's Monthly, in the first
         reference.
         Click the Underline button on the Formatting toolbar.
         Select the text, Internet Research Journal, in the
         second reference.
         Click the Underline button on the Formatting toolbar.
         Select the text, Creating a Working Bibliography, in
         the third reference.
         Click the Underline button on the Formatting toolbar.

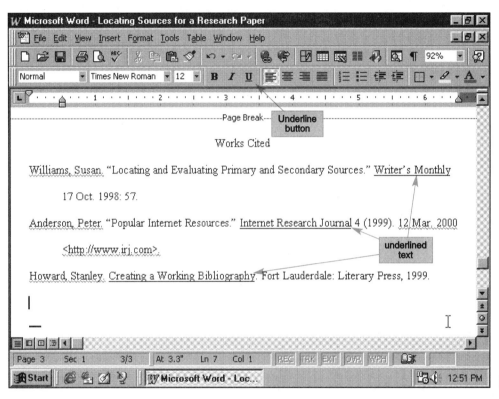

Figure 70

The magazine name (Writer's Monthly) in the first reference, journal name (Internet Research Journal) in the second reference, and book name (Creating a Working Bibliography) in the third reference are underlined.

Sorting the References

Next, select and sort the three references in the Works Cited list. Perform the following steps to select and sort the references.

Step 1 **Point to the margin to the left of the first line in the first reference.**

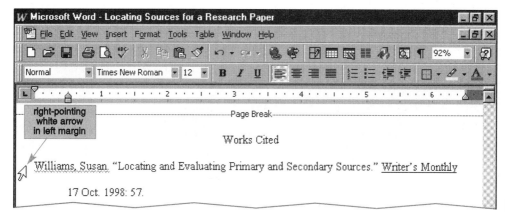

Figure 71

When you move the mouse pointer into the left margin, the mouse pointer changes to a right-pointing white arrow. The mouse pointer points to the first line of the first reference.

Step 2 **Drag the mouse pointer down the left margin to select the three references.**

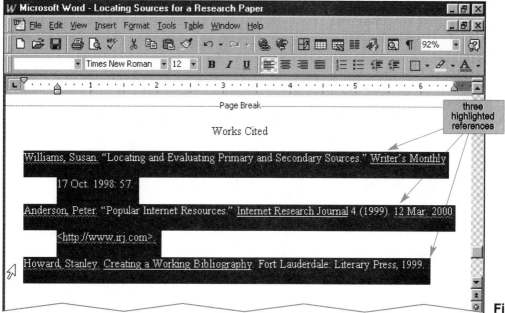

Figure 72

Word selects the three references.

Step 3 Click Table on the menu bar.
Point to the Sort command on the Table menu.

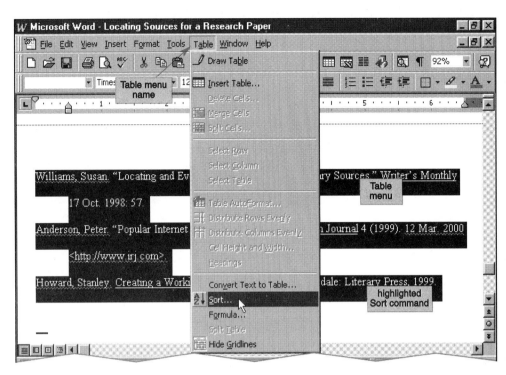

Figure 73

The Table menu displays, and the mouse pointer points to the highlighted Sort command.

Step 4 Click the Sort command.
Point to the OK button in the Sort Text dialog box.

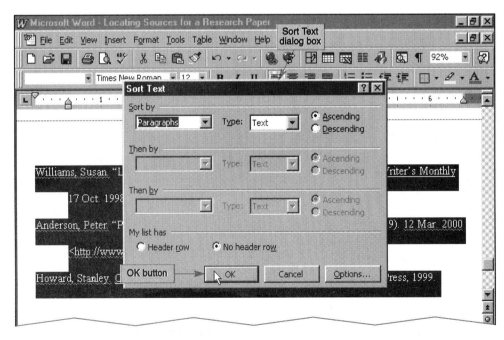

Figure 74

The Sort Text dialog box, containing the settings to sort the paragraphs in ascending order, displays. The mouse pointer points to the OK button.

Step 5   Click the OK button.
          Click the blank line below the third reference to
              remove the highlight and position the insertion
              point on the blank line.

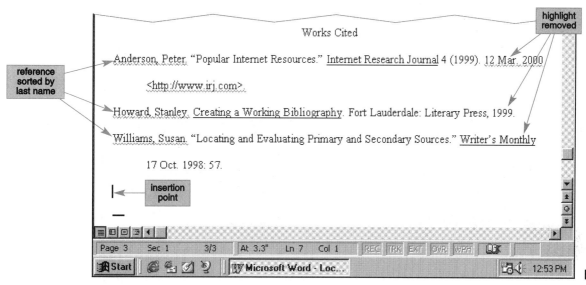

reference
sorted by
last name

highlight
removed

Works Cited

Anderson, Peter. "Popular Internet Resources." Internet Research Journal 4 (1999). 12 Mar. 2000

<http://www.irj.com>.

Howard, Stanley. Creating a Working Bibliography. Fort Lauderdale: Literary Press, 1999.

Williams, Susan. "Locating and Evaluating Primary and Secondary Sources." Writer's Monthly

17 Oct. 1998: 57.

insertion
point

Page 3   Sec 1   3/3   At 3.3"   Ln 7   Col 1   REC TRK EXT OVR WPH

Start   Microsoft Word - Loc...   12:53 PM

Figure 75

Word sorts the references alphabetically by the last name of the author.

Saving the Modified Research Paper

After completing the research paper, save the research paper again using the Save button on the Formatting toolbar and the same file name (Locating Sources for a Research Paper). The following steps save the completed research paper.

Step 1   **Point to the Save button on the Standard toolbar.**

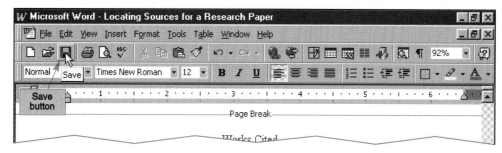

Microsoft Word - Locating Sources for a Research Paper

File   Edit   View   Insert   Format   Tools   Table   Window   Help

Normal   Times New Roman   12   B   I   U

Save

Save
button

Page Break

Works Cited

Figure 76

The mouse pointer points to the Save button.

Step 2   **Click the Save button.**

Word saves the document on the floppy disk in drive A using the Locating Sources for a Research Paper file name.

Printing the Research Paper

After completing the research paper, you may wish to print the paper. A printed copy of a document is called a **printout**. The following steps print the research paper.

Step 1 Point to the Print button on the Standard toolbar.

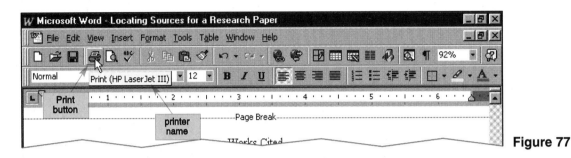

Figure 77

The mouse pointer points to the Print button, and a ScreenTip displays.
The ScreenTip contains the printer name (HP LaserJet III).

Step 2 Click the Print button.

The research paper illustrated in Figure 1 on pages 2 and 3 prints on the printer.

When you use the Print button to print a multiple-page document, Word prints all the pages in the document. If you wish to print a single page or a range of pages, click File on the menu bar, click the Print command, click the Pages text box in the Print dialog box, type a single page number (2) or a page range (2-3) in the text box, and click the OK button.

After printing the research paper, you can use the printout to proofread the research paper. In addition, you may want to determine the number of words in the research paper and make changes to the paper based upon the word count. The next section illustrates how to determine the number of words in a document.

Determining the Word Count

Often your teacher will specify the number of words the research paper can contain. The research paper in this book is a relatively short paper containing approximately 500 words. After printing the research paper and before proofreading the paper, you should determine if you are close to the number of words allowed by your teacher. The following steps check the word count of the research paper.

Step 1 Click Tools on the menu bar.
Point to the Word Count command on the Tools menu.

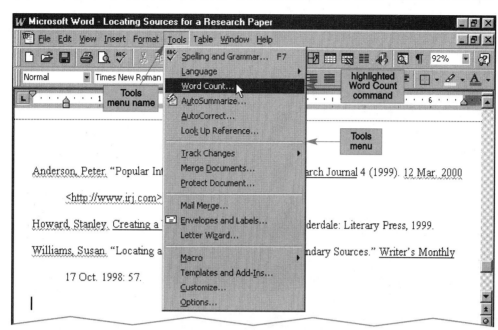

Figure 78

The Tools menu displays, and the mouse pointer points to the highlighted Word Count command.

Step 2 Click the Word Count command.
If a check mark does not display in the Include footnotes and endnotes check box, click the check box to place a check mark in it.
Point to the Close button in the Word Count dialog box.

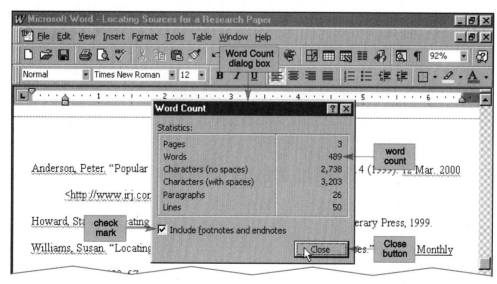

Figure 79

Word opens the Word Count dialog box. The dialog box contains the number of pages, words, characters, paragraphs, and lines in the paper. These numbers change when you click the Include footnotes and endnotes check box. Currently, the research paper contains 489 words.

Step 3   Click the Close button.

The Word Count dialog box closes.

You can use the word count to guarantee that the number of words in the research paper meets the word count requirement of your teacher.

Quitting Microsoft Word 97

After creating, saving, printing, and determining the word count of the research paper, you have finished using Microsoft Word and should quit Word. Perform the following steps to quit Microsoft Word.

Step 1   Point to the Close button in the Microsoft Word - Locating Sources for a Research Paper window.

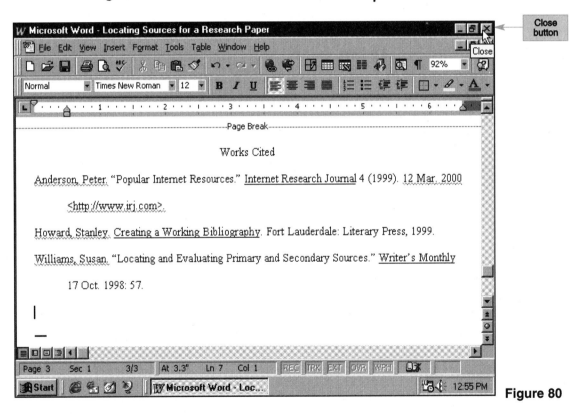

Figure 80

The mouse pointer points to the Close button.

Step 2   Click the Close button.

The Microsoft Word program quits, the Microsoft Word window closes, and the Windows desktop displays.

The research paper is now complete. The next section in this book shows you how to make changes to the research paper. Making changes often involves scrolling a document, finding a specific page or a word on a page, inserting and deleting text, using the Word Thesaurus, and spell and grammar checking. To make changes to your research paper, proceed to the next section of this book.

Editing a Research Paper

After printing the research paper and before turning in the paper to your teacher, you should check your research paper for errors. Although some writers like to read a research paper on the screen, it is best to print the research paper by performing the steps on page 58, making changes on the printed copy, and then entering any changes to the research paper on the computer. In computer terminology, the process of changing the content of a document is referred to as **editing the document**.

Revising the Research Paper

In the process of writing a research paper, you will make many changes to the paper. One stage in the development of a research paper that requires making changes to the paper is the revision process. **Revising** involves checking the quality of writing in the research paper. You might ask yourself if the paper achieves its original purpose, if the audience understands the topic of the paper, if every paragraph has a central idea, and if detail or examples would be helpful. Many writers get others to read the paper to obtain feedback and helpful advice. In a school environment, you might ask another student to read your paper, visit the writing center to talk with a tutor, or conference with your teacher. Revising the research paper often results in large-scale changes to the paper.

Editing and Proofreading the Research Paper

Another stage in the development of a research paper that requires making changes to the paper is the editing process. **Editing** involves checking for proper grammar, punctuation, spelling, and usage. The best time to edit the paper is after making the larger changes often associated with revising the paper. Editing often results in small-scale changes to the paper.

Next, you should proofread the paper. **Proofreading** involves checking for missing words, misspellings, and format requirements. While proofreading the research paper, look for spelling and grammatical errors, check for the proper use of the MLA guidelines, double-check each parenthetical citation and its reference for accuracy, and look for ways to improve readability.

Proofreading is the final step before turning in the finished research paper to your teacher. You should read the research paper slowly and check each letter of each word. Suggestions for proofreading include reading from right to left instead of left to right, using a pencil to point to each word as you say the word aloud, and placing a piece of paper under the line you are reading. Proofread the document a second time from the beginning to end and concentrate on each sentence, its meaning, and the words in the sentence. Proofreading often results in changes to the paper.

Opening the Research Paper Document

After revising, editing, and proofreading the research paper, you will have to start Microsoft Word and retrieve the research paper from the floppy disk in drive A to edit the research paper.

The following steps illustrate how to start Microsoft Word and retrieve the Locating Sources for a Research Paper document from the floppy disk in drive A.

Step 1 Click the Start button on the taskbar.
Point to the Open Office Document command on
the Start menu.

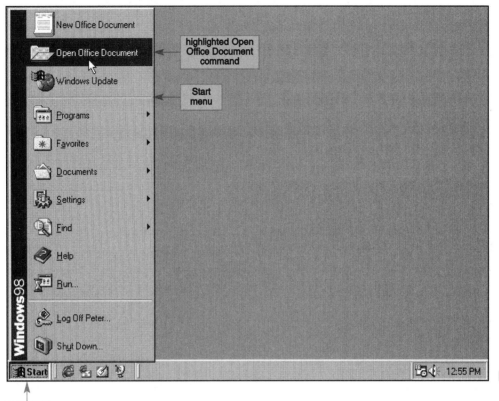

Figure 81

The Start menu displays, and the mouse pointer points to the highlighted
Open Office Document command.

Step 2 Click the Open Office Document command.
Click the down arrow button in the Look in
drop-down list box.
Click the 3½ Floppy (A:) drive name in the Look in
drop-down list.
Click the Locating Sources for a Research Paper file
name in the list box.
Point to the Open button.

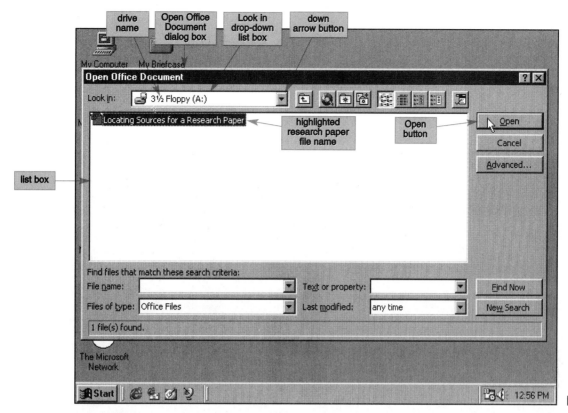

Figure 82

The Open Office Document dialog box opens, the 3½ Floppy (A:) drive name displays in the Look in drop-down list box, the highlighted Locating Sources for a Research Paper file name displays in the list box, and the mouse pointer points to the Open button. The list box on your computer may contain additional file names.

Step 3   Click the Open button.

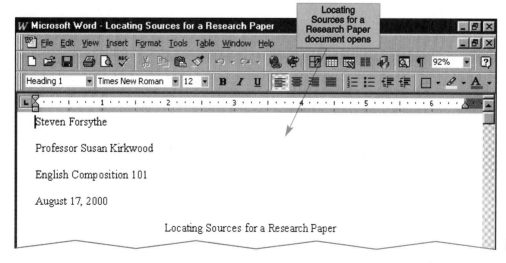

Figure 83

The Open Office Document dialog box closes, Word starts, and Word retrieves the Locating Sources for a Research Paper document from the floppy disk in drive A and displays the document in the Microsoft Word window.

After opening the research paper, you can make changes to the Locating Sources for a Research Paper document based upon the changes you made to the printout of the research paper. To make these changes, you may have to: 1) scroll a document window; 2) browse for an object; 3) search for text; 4) insert, replace, and delete text; and 5) undo a previously performed operation. The following sections explain how to perform these tasks.

Scrolling a Document

As mentioned previously, scroll bars display when an entire document is not completely visible in a window. A vertical scroll bar contains an up scroll arrow, a down scroll arrow, and a scroll box (see Figure 6 on page 8). Similarly, a horizontal scroll bar contains a left scroll arrow, a right scroll arrow, and a scroll box.

You can use the scroll arrows, scroll bar, and scroll box on the vertical scroll bar to view areas of the document that are not visible in the text area. The table below summarizes the various ways you can scroll a document using the vertical scroll bar. Refer to this table as needed to scroll the document.

WAYS TO SCROLL	ACTION REQUIRED
Scroll a window up and move the text down one line.	Click the up scroll arrow.
Scroll a window down and move the text up one line.	Click the down scroll arrow.
Continuously scroll a window up.	Point to the up scroll arrow and hold down the left mouse button.
Continuously scroll a window down.	Point to the down scroll arrow and hold down the left mouse button.
Scroll a window down one screen.	Click the scroll bar above the scroll box.
Scroll a window up one screen.	Click the scroll bar below the scroll box.
Scroll toward the top of a document.	Drag the scroll box up.
Scroll toward the bottom of a document.	Drag the scroll box down.

Table 2

You can also use the scroll arrows, scroll bar, and scroll box on the horizontal scroll bar in a similar manner to move the text in a document horizontally.

Scrolling the Research Paper

Although you can scroll by using the scroll arrows or scroll bar, using the scroll box allows you to quickly move long distances within a document. The following steps illustrate how to scroll a document using the scroll box.

Step 1 Point to the scroll box on the vertical scroll bar.
Hold down the left mouse button.

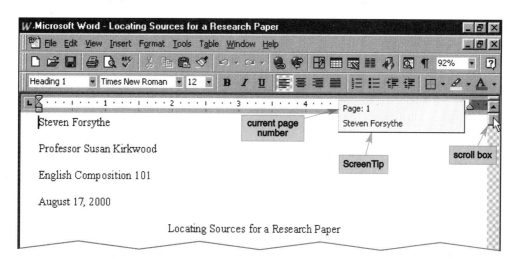

Figure 84

When you hold down the left mouse button, a ScreenTip displays that
contains the current page number (1) and author's name (Steven Forsythe).

Step 2 Drag the scroll box downward along the scroll bar until
the page number in the ScreenTip changes to 3.
Release the left mouse button.
Click the blank line at the bottom of the page to
position the insertion point on the blank line.

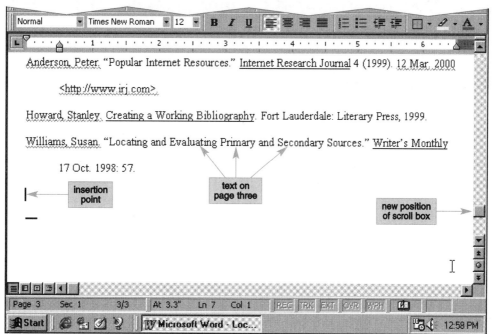

Figure 85

The scroll box changes position, a portion of page three displays, and the
insertion point displays at the bottom of the page.

Browsing a Document for a Specific Page

In addition to scrolling, you may use other methods to move within a document. One method uses the Select Browse Object button at the bottom of the vertical scroll bar to browse for an object (page, footnote, table, etc.) in a document. The following steps illustrate how to browse through the pages of the research paper.

Step 1 Click the Select Browse Object button on the vertical scroll bar.
Point to the Browse by Page command (upper right corner) in the Select Browse Object menu.

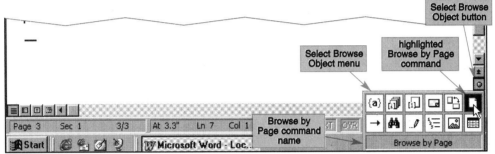

Figure 86

The Select Browse Object menu displays. The mouse pointer points to the highlighted Browse by Page command, and the command name, Browse by Page, displays at the bottom of the menu.

Step 2 Click the Browse by Page command.
Point to the Previous Page button above the Select Browse Object button.

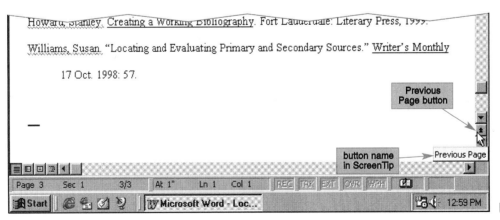

Figure 87

The Select Browse Object menu disappears. When you point to the Previous Page button, a ScreenTip containing the button name (Previous Page) displays. The button name changes depending upon the command you choose in the Select Browse Object menu.

Step 3 **Click the Previous Page button twice.**

The top of page one displays and the insertion point is located at the top of the document.

Finding Text in a Document

Another method to move within a document is to use the Select Browse Object button and the Find command to search for a word in a document. The following steps search for the word, bibliography, in the research paper.

Step 1 **Click the Select Browse Object button on the vertical scroll bar.**
Point to the Find command in the Select Browse Object menu.

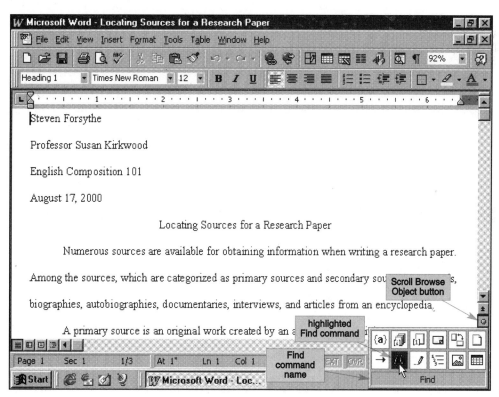

Figure 88

The Select Browse Object menu displays, the mouse pointer points to the highlighted Find command, and the command name, Find, displays at the bottom of the menu.

Step 2   Click the Find command.
Type **bibliography** in the Find what drop-down list box
        in the Find and Replace dialog box.
Point to the Find Next button in the dialog box.

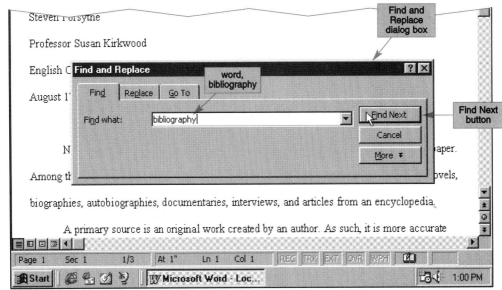

Figure 89

The Select Browse Object menu disappears, and the word, bibliography,
displays in the Find what drop-down list box. The mouse pointer points to the
Find Next button.

Step 3   Click the Find Next button.
Point to the Close button in the Find and Replace
        dialog box.

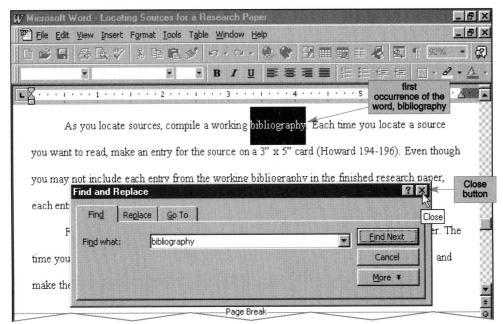

Figure 90

When you click the Find Next button, Word finds and highlights the first
occurrence of the word, bibliography, in the document. The mouse pointer
points to the Close button.

Step 4 **Click the Close button.**

Clicking the Close button closes the Find and Replace dialog box. The word, bibliography, remains highlighted.

Clicking the Find Next button a second time displays the second occurrence of the word, bibliography, in the document.

Finding and Replacing a Word

You can also find and replace text within a document using the same technique as finding a word. When the Find and Replace dialog box opens, click the Replace tab to display the Replace with drop-down list box, enter a word or phrase in the Find what drop-down list box, enter a replacement word or phrase in the Replace with drop-down list box, and click the Find Next button to find the first occurrence of the word. Clicking the Replace button replaces the word with its replacement word. Clicking the Replace All button replaces all occurrences of the word in the document with its replacement word.

Editing the Research Paper

The next step in revising the research paper is to use the techniques of scrolling, browsing, and finding to make the changes to the text in the research paper. Typically, the changes you make to a research paper involve inserting, deleting, or replacing text. The following section explains how to insert and replace text in a research paper.

Inserting and Replacing Text

In **insert mode**, when you type from the keyboard, the text to the right of the insertion point moves to the right and downward to accommodate the new text. Insert mode is the **default typing mode**. Thus, to insert text in a document, you position the insertion point where you want to insert the text and type the new text. While in insert mode, the **OVR status indicator** on the status bar contains the dimmed OVR characters (see Figure 6 on page 8).

In **overtype mode**, when you press a key on the keyboard, the character associated with the key replaces the character to the right of the insertion point. In this case, the new text replaces the text on the screen. While in overtype mode, the OVR status indicator on the status bar contains the highlighted OVR characters.

You switch between modes by pressing the INSERT (INS) key on the keyboard.

Deleting Text

In addition to inserting and replacing text, you also should know how to delete text. The table on the next page summarizes the various ways you can delete text in a document. Refer to this table as needed to delete text.

TO DELETE	ACTION TO BE PERFORMED
The character to the right of the insertion point	Press the DELETE key.
The character to the left of the insertion point	Press the BACKSPACE key.
A word or series of words	Select the word or words, and press the DELETE key.
A word to the left of the insertion point	Position the insertion point in the blank space to the right of the word, hold down the CTRL key, and press the BACKSPACE key.
A word to the right of the insertion point	Position the insertion point in the blank space to the left of the word, hold down the CTRL key, and press the DELETE key.
A table	Click any cell in the table, click Table on the menu bar, point to the Delete command, and click the Table command.

Table 3

Undoing and Redoing a Previously Performed Operation

In the process of inserting, deleting, and replacing text, you may decide that you want to reverse the last operation you performed. For example, you may have changed the research paper by inserting a new sentence in the paper. To reverse this operation and remove the sentence, click the Undo button on the Standard toolbar. If, after using Undo to remove the sentence, you decide you want the sentence back in the paper, click the Redo button on the Standard toolbar. The table below summarizes how to undo and redo an operation. Refer to this table as needed to undo and redo operations.

OPERATION	ACTION TO BE PERFORMED
Undo your most recent operation	Press the Undo button on the Standard toolbar.
Undo a series of operations	Press the down arrow button on the Undo button, and click the last operation in the list you want to undo.
Cancel your most recent undo operation	Press the Redo button on the Standard toolbar.
Cancel a series of your most recent undo operations	Press the down arrow button on the Redo button, and click the last operation in the list you want to cancel.

Table 4

In addition to working with text, the Undo button also allows you to reverse a variety of other operations, including reversing the creation of a header or footnote, centering of text, and changing the page margins, font size, and line spacing. You cannot reverse operations such as saving and printing a document.

Using the Word Thesaurus

When writing a research paper, it is easy to thoughtlessly use the same word multiple times and then later find you wish to use a variety of words. You may also find that you want to replace a word with a more meaningful word. Using Word, you can replace any word with a word of similar meaning, called a **synonym**, or a word of opposite meaning, called an **antonym**. A dictionary of synonyms and antonyms, called a **thesaurus**, is included with Microsoft Word. The following steps use the Word Thesaurus to replace the word, Finally, in the last paragraph of the research paper with a word with a similar meaning.

Step 1 Position the insertion point in the word, Finally, in the last paragraph.
Click Tools on the menu bar.
Point to the Language command on the Tools menu.
Point to the Thesaurus command on the Language menu.

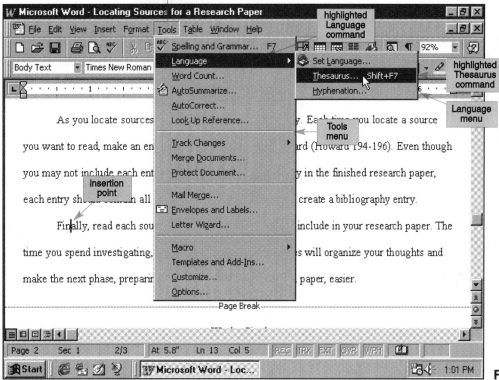

Figure 91

The insertion point is located in the word, Finally, the Tools menu displays, and the highlighted Thesaurus command displays in the Language menu.

Step 2   **Click the Thesaurus command.**
        Click the synonym, in conclusion, in the Replace with
           Synonym list box.
        Point to the Replace button.

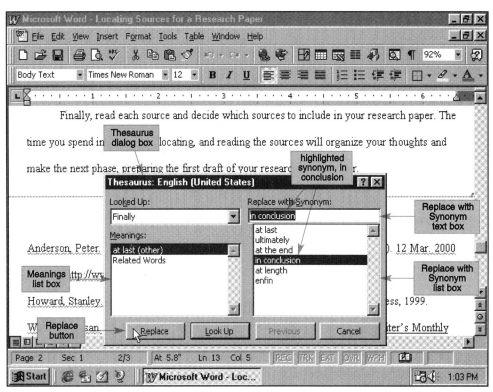

Figure 92

The Thesaurus: English (United States) dialog box opens. The different meanings of the selected word (Finally) display in the Meanings list box, and the synonyms for the selected word display in the Replace with Synonym list box. The highlighted synonym, in conclusion, displays in the Replace with Synonym text box and list box.

Step 3   **Click the Replace button.**

The synonym, In conclusion, replaces the word, Finally, in the research paper.

Spell Checking the Research Paper Again

    As mentioned previously, if a jagged red line displays below a word you type, the word may not be in the Word dictionary. To find a replacement for the word, right-click the word to display a shortcut menu of replacement words, and then click a replacement word from the shortcut menu to replace the incorrectly spelled word.

    After you proofread and revise the research paper, you should scan the research paper for red or green jagged lines and fix each incorrectly spelled word or grammar problem.

    Alternatively, you can spell and grammar check the entire research paper at one time. Although this book does not contain the steps to accomplish this, the next section on the Office Assistant explains how to use the Help feature to learn more about spell checking.

Saving and Printing the Research Paper

After completing the additional work on the research paper, save the research paper and print it using the steps shown on pages 57 and 58.

Using the Office Assistant to Obtain Help

If you have a question while using Microsoft Word, you can use Help to get an answer to your question. Although there are many different ways to obtain help while using Microsoft Word, one of the easiest methods is to use the **Office Assistant**. To use the Office Assistant, you type in a word, phrase, or question, and Word displays a list of related help topics. Perform the following steps to view a help topic about spell and grammar checking.

Step 1   If the Office Assistant does not display on the screen, click the Office Assistant button on the Standard toolbar.
Type **how do I spell check** in the text box in the Assistant balloon.
Point to the Search button.

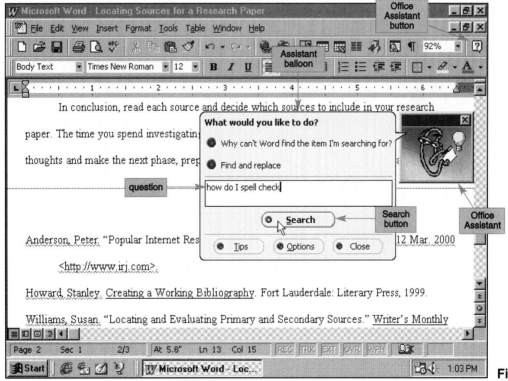

Figure 93

The Office Assistant displays on the screen. The Office Assistant consists of an animated paper clip and the Assistant balloon. The balloon contains a text box to enter a word, phrase, or question and four buttons (Search, Tips, Options, and Close). The question, how do I spell check, and the insertion point display in the text box. The mouse pointer points to the Search button.

Step 2   Click the Search button.
   Point to the Correct spelling and grammar topic in
      the Assistant balloon.

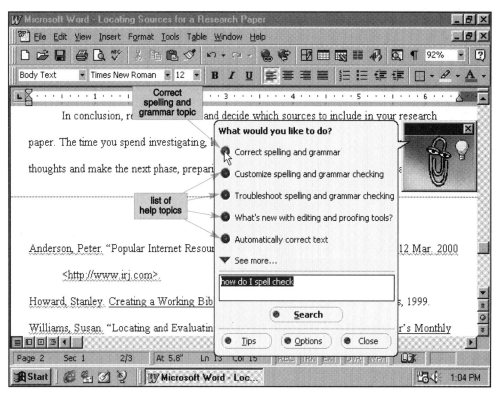

Figure 94

A list of help topics displays in the Assistant balloon. The mouse pointer
points to the Correct spelling and grammar topic.

Step 3   Click the Correct spelling and grammar topic.
   Point to the second button (Check spelling,
      grammar, and readability all at once) in the
      Microsoft Word window.

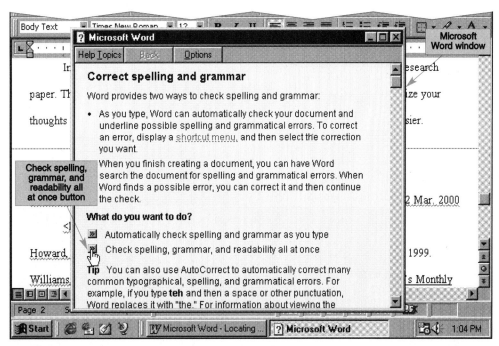

Figure 95

The Microsoft Word window opens. Two buttons identified by two right arrows display. The mouse pointer points to the second button (Check spelling, grammar, and readability all at once) in the window.

Step 4 **Click the second button.**
Scroll the Microsoft Word window to read the help topic.

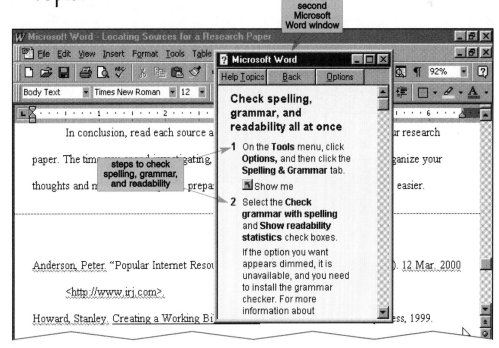

Figure 96

Another Microsoft Word window, containing the steps to check spelling, grammar, and readability all at once, opens. Scrolling the window allows you to view the steps to spell check the entire research paper at one time.

Step 5   When you have completed reading the help topic,
click the Close button in the Microsoft Word
window.
Click the Close button in the Office Assistant.

The Microsoft Word and Office Assistant windows close.

Quitting Microsoft Word 97

When you have finished using Microsoft Word, quit Word by performing the following steps.

Step 1   Click the Close button in the Microsoft Word -
Locating Sources for a Research Paper window.

Step 2   If you have made changes to the research paper
since the last time you saved the paper, a
Microsoft Word dialog box opens to prompt you
to save the changes before you quit Word.
Click the Yes button to save changes, or click the
No button if you do not wish to save the
changes.

The Microsoft Word program quits, and the Microsoft Word window closes.

Conclusion

In this book, you created and edited a sample research paper. You learned about the Microsoft Windows operating system, MLA style guidelines, and default Microsoft Word settings. You used Microsoft Word 97 to change page margins, zoom setting, font size, line spacing, and text justification. You created a header (running head), typed parenthetical citations and a footnote, inserted a table, inserted a hard page break, spell and grammar checked the paper, used the Thesaurus, created the Works Cited list using a hanging indent, performed a word count, and saved and printed the paper. In addition, you learned to select text, insert and delete text, scroll a window, browse through a document, undo and redo previous operations, and use the Word Help system.

Whether you followed the steps in this book to create the sample research paper illustrated in the book or to create your own research paper, you now have an understanding of how to create MLA style research papers. We hope this book has made the process easier for you, and we encourage you to visit our Web site (www.stevenspress.com) for further information.

Appendixes

Appendix A

MLA Style Guidelines and Word Default Settings

Appendix B

General Steps to Create a Research Paper

Appendix A - MLA Style Guidelines and Word Default Settings

The Modern Language Association (MLA) maintains the MLA documentation style, or MLA style, guidelines. The table below contains the research paper feature, MLA guideline, Microsoft Word default setting, and the steps to change the default setting to conform to the MLA style guideline.

Research Paper Feature	MLA Guideline	Microsoft Word Default Setting	Steps to Change Default Setting to Conform to MLA Guideline
Page Margins	All margins are one-inch	Left and right (1.25"), top and bottom (1")	Click Page Setup on the File menu
Header Spacing	One-half inch	.5"	No change required
Header Justification	Right justified	Left justification	Click Header and Footer on View menu, click Align Right button on Formatting toolbar, type header, click Close button
Font and Font Size	Font and font size should be readable	Times New Roman and 10 point	Click down arrow button on Font drop-down list box or Font Size drop-down list box, click font name or font size
Line Spacing	Double spaced	Single spacing	Click Paragraph on Format menu, click down arrow button on Line spacing drop-down list box, click double
Text Justification	Left justified	Left justification	No change required
Title Page	Title page not required	None	Type name and course information
Research Paper Title	Centered	Left justification	Click Center button on Formatting toolbar
Paragraph Indentation	One-half inch	.5"	Press the TAB key
Documenting References	Use parenthetical citations	None	Type parenthetical citations
Parenthetical Citation Format	Author last name, blank space, and date or page reference enclosed in parentheses	None	Type parenthetical citation in parentheses
Footnote	Indent footnote one-half inch, single space, double space between footnotes, same font and font size as body	No indentation, single spacing, Times New Roman font, and 10 point font size	Click Footnote on Insert menu, click OK button, press HOME key, press TAB key, press END key, set font size to 12 point
Table	Place close to reference, type label, caption, and source	None	Click Insert Table button on Standard toolbar, click cell on table grid to set table size
Works Cited List	Separate page with header, centered title, references indented alphabetical order by author's last name	Left justified, no hanging indent	Click Break on Insert menu, click OK button, type and center title, drag Hanging Indent button to .5" mark on ruler, type and select references, click Sort on Table menu, click OK button

Appendix B - General Steps to Create a Research Paper

Appendix B contains a list of the general steps to follow to word process an MLA style research paper using Microsoft Word 97. Remember to spell check and grammar check as you type the research paper.

General Steps to Word Process a Research Paper

1. Start Microsoft Windows (turn on the computer).
2. Start Microsoft Word.
3. Change the left and right margins.
4. Change the zoom setting.
5. Change the font size.
6. Change the line spacing.
7. Create the header (running head).
8. Type the name and course information.
9. Type and center the research paper title.
10. Type the body of the research paper. Indent each paragraph.
11. Type parenthetical citations as required.
12. Save the research paper.
13. Type footnotes as required.
14. Insert tables as required. Insert a blank line following the table.
15. Create the Works Cited page by inserting a manual page break.
16. Type and center the Works Cited title.
17. Create a hanging indent and type the references.
18. Sort the references on the Works Cited page.
19. Save the modified research paper.
20. Print the research paper.
21. Determine the word count for the research paper.
22. Revise, edit, and proofread the research paper.
23. Edit (change) the research paper.
24. Spell and grammar check the research paper.
25. Save and print the research paper.
26. Quit Microsoft Word.
27. Turn off the computer.

INDEX